Starting A Small Business

From Scratch to Success - Turning Napkin Doodles into A Booming Business

Lee Merritt

Contents

Introduction: From Couch Dreamer to Business Schemer

My rollercoaster ride in the business world

Starting a business often feels like standing at the foot of a majestic mountain. The summit calls out, tempting with its allure, yet the path upward is hidden by fog, laden with unforeseen challenges and surprises. I know this landscape well; it's been my playground and battlefield for the last two decades.

Gazing up, it's easy to feel daunted, wondering if you have the endurance to navigate the steep inclines or the resilience to weather the storms that might brew. But with each step, the journey unfolds lessons more valuable than gold. For every stumble, there's a newfound strength; for every detour, a hidden gem of insight waiting to be discovered. My name is Lee, and I've summited these entrepreneurial peaks, faced the blizzards, basked in the sunlit clearings, and pitched my tent under the canopy of stars during the darkest nights. This book is my trail map for you, a guide through the terrains I've traversed, so you can chart your own path with confidence and vision.

After that initial climb, my ventures felt like a series of interconnected trails. My first endeavor was a retail store, right in the heart of a bustling town. The excitement of opening day, the aroma of fresh paint, the uncertainty of the first sale — it was all intoxicating. But, much like an unexpected downpour on a mountain trek, I faced challenges. Inventory mishaps hit me, a flood wreaked havoc in the store during the very first year, and amidst all this, grasping the nuances of the local market became a puzzle of its own.

However, with each challenge came invaluable insights. The flood underscored the necessity of having robust insurance and a backup plan. The inventory glitches pushed me to delve into the intricacies of supply chain management, forging relationships that would stand me in good stead in later ventures. And trying to navigate the local market? It taught me the significance of community engagement and understanding local consumer behavior, shaping my approach for future business strategies.

Next came an online platform, a step into the then-emerging world of digital markets. This was akin to navigating a forest at night. The world of SEO, digital advertising, and user experience was new and bewildering. But, with tenacity, I began to decipher the patterns, understanding the rhythms of this digital jungle. It also led to my first major success, turning the venture profitable within a year and expanding internationally.

However, not every expedition reached its intended destination. An attempt to introduce an innovative organic food product hit regulatory roadblocks. It felt like reaching a cliff on my hike — insurmountable and ending the path I had been on. Yet, it was also a lesson in patience, research, and understanding the nuances of the business landscape.

These experiences, and countless others, form the mosaic of my entrepreneurial journey. Through this book, I don't just share strategies or market analyses; I offer the raw, unfiltered tales from the trenches. The aim? To equip you with both knowledge and spirit, so as you embark on your journey, you do so with a seasoned traveler's wisdom and a beginner's enthusiasm.

Now, as we set forth into the nitty-gritty of starting a small business, know that with every chapter, with every page, you're not just reading a guide — you're gaining a companion for your own incredible journey. Let's make it a story worth telling.

Why Entrepreneurship is the Ultimate Adventure

Ah, adventures! They come in all shapes and sizes. Some of us crave the thrill of skydiving, others find joy in the quiet discovery of a new book or cuisine. But let me tell you, if life's experiences had an Olympics, entrepreneurship would be that electrifying decathlon where every event tests a different facet of your being.

Firstly, much like any grand quest, entrepreneurship starts with a vision. Think of the explorers of old, setting out with maps and compasses, venturing into the unknown. They had uncharted territories, we have our dreams. That tantalizing idea that won't let you sleep, the vision of a product or service that fills a gap in the market - that's your uncharted territory, your beginning.

Now, I won't sugarcoat it. This path is not a straight, paved highway. It's more akin to the winding trails of the Grand Canyon, filled with ups, downs, and mesmerizing views. One day you're the captain of a ship sailing smoothly, and the next, you're battling tempestuous seas, hoping your vessel withstands the storm.

There's the thrill of the first 1000 sales, akin to reaching a mountaintop and seeing the world spread out beneath you. There's the puzzle-solving joy when you finally crack a marketing strategy or optimize a supply chain issue – it's that "Eureka!" moment in a dimly lit cave, unearthing a hidden artifact.

Yet, with the highs come the lows. The failed product launch, or that one month where numbers just won't add up. These moments? They're your dense forests, your quicksand, the moments where every step feels ten times harder. But it's in these moments, dear reader, that the mettle of an entrepreneur is tested and often, where the most profound lessons are learned.

And let's not forget our companions along the way. Just as any legendary hero had their loyal sidekicks – think Batman and Robin, or Sherlock and Watson – entrepreneurs too have their mentors, partners, and teams. They bring in perspectives you might miss, lift your spirits when the journey gets tough, and celebrate the milestones, big and small.

But perhaps the most exhilarating aspect of this adventure? It's uniquely yours. While there might be thousands of coffee shops or tech startups, no two entrepreneurial stories are the same. Each venture, each challenge, each success, and each stumble writes a chapter in a tale that is singularly yours.

In this book, I'll share the tools you'll need, the mindset to adopt, and the strategies that can propel you forward. But remember, while the framework might be similar, it's the personal touches, the individual choices, and the unique challenges that will make your entrepreneurial story truly memorable.

So, strap on your boots, grab your metaphorical map, and let's embark on one of the greatest adventures of your life. It's time to chart the uncharted, dream the undreamt, and build the unimagined.

The Game Plan for This Book

Imagine, if you will, that you've stumbled upon a secret map — one that promises a treasure but demands a thrilling quest. Well, this book is precisely that map, and the treasure? Your successful business!

We'll kick things off by tapping into that fiery entrepreneurial spirit. Think of it like lighting the torch that'll guide us through the journey ahead.

Next, we plunge into the idea pool, where waves of innovation and vision await. At times, you might feel you're merely treading water, but with each stroke, clarity emerges, propelling you forward. And yes, every quest has its dragons. Ours? Doubts, fears, and rookie blunders. But fret not; I've armed this book with strategies and insights that'll help you conquer them all.

Emerging from the waters of ideation, we gear up for an ascent. Crafting your business plan, securing funds, and laying the foundation of your empire will resemble a climb up a challenging peak. Yet, equipped with the tools and tactics within these pages, you won't just scale the mountain; you'll stake your claim at its pinnacle, marking your territory in the market landscape.

Our journey then steers us through the realms of positioning and pricing. Here, you'll master the craft of distinction, ensuring your business isn't lost in the masses but stands as a lighthouse, guiding customers to its shores.

The concluding chapters guide us through the vibrant avenues of marketing, leading onto the adaptable pathways of business expansion. It's not just strategy; it's a rhythm, an evolving heartbeat that ensures your business doesn't just survive but thrives.

As you navigate this guide, every word, tip, and anecdote is a beacon on your entrepreneurial path. Together, we'll journey through the intricacies of business, and I'm here with you every step of the way. Let's transform your visions into victories, one chapter at a time!

Part I: Laying the Foundation: Validating Ideas and Cultivating a Winning Mindset

Chapter One

Embracing the Entrepreneurial Spirit

Small Business 101: More than just a tiny shop

Now, before you start imagining yourself flipping the 'Open' sign on your front door, let's get a couple of things straight. A 'small business' isn't defined by its square footage or the number of espresso machines it houses. It's characterized by its spirit — the soulful energy that makes customers feel at home and employees feel valued.

But why, you ask, would anyone dive into the turbulent waters of entrepreneurship when the serene shores of a 9-to-5 job await? It's not just about building something; it's about ownership. Being the captain of your ship means setting its course, weathering storms, and basking in the sunny days that follow.

Remember the magic of unwrapping a gift as a kid? That mix of anticipation, excitement, and the sheer thrill of discovery? Starting a small business gifts you that feeling — but on steroids. Every challenge you tackle, every customer you delight, every product you launch... they're all wrapped in that same magical paper.

Now, don't get me wrong. This isn't some starry-eyed view of entrepreneurship where every day ends with a fairy tale sunset. There'll be times when you wonder if you're cut out for this, days where the weight of responsibility feels immense. But amidst those moments, there'll be instances of sheer joy, of unbridled passion, of the realization that you're doing something bigger than just turning a profit.

I've seen both sides of the coin. I've basked in the applause and grappled with the silence. And through it all, I've realized one undeniable truth: every small business, at its core, is a manifestation of an entrepreneurial spirit that refuses to be boxed in by definitions. It's not just a tiny shop or a quaint café. It's a beacon of hope, of ambition, of dreams taking flight.

So, as you embark on this journey, remember to look beyond the brick and mortar, beyond the numbers and the spreadsheets. Embrace the spirit, the fire that fuels your passion. For in doing so, you're not just starting a business; you're crafting a legacy.

The Rollercoaster of the Entrepreneurial Mind: Ups, Downs, and Loop-de-Loops

If I could paint a picture of the entrepreneurial mind, I'd depict a rollercoaster—sometimes exhilarating, sometimes gut-wrenching, always unforgettable. Strap in, because understanding this rollercoaster is crucial to navigating the wild ride of starting your own venture.

Let's start with the uphill climb. This is that phase where everything is exciting. The possibilities seem endless, and the sky isn't even the limit—perhaps Mars is! It's when you're burning the midnight oil, scribbling ideas on napkins, or talking animatedly about your vision to anyone who'll listen.

But, like any rollercoaster, after the climb often comes a dip. Maybe your first prototype flopped. Maybe a key partner backed out. Or perhaps that "guaranteed" market strategy didn't pan out as expected. Suddenly, gravity feels stronger, and self-doubt tries to buckle you in tighter.

But remember: after the dip, rollercoasters have their loop-de-loops. These are the twisty turns of entrepreneurship—those moments of unexpected pivot, where a challenge flips into an opportunity. It's when you innovate on the fly, discovering new facets of your business or market you hadn't considered. Here, agility is your best buddy.

Then there are the straight paths—those rare, sweet moments of smooth sailing. Sales are up, feedback is glowing, and everything is humming along. It's tempting to relax and enjoy the wind in your hair. But remember, on this ride, complacency can be the silent track-switcher that derails you.

Lastly, the scenic points. These are the milestones, big or small, that remind you of why you started this wild ride in the first place. Maybe it's a heartfelt thank-you note from a satisfied customer, or perhaps the moment you ship out your 100th product. These points are your photo ops—snapshots to cherish and fuel your journey ahead.

Throughout this rollercoaster, you'll need two things: a sturdy safety harness (your core values and mission) and an eager hand ready to throw up in sheer excitement. Because, let's be real, the best rollercoasters aren't the ones that are smooth and predictable. They're the ones that surprise you, challenge you, and leave you breathlessly waiting for another go.

So, as you buckle up for this ride, remember: every twist, turn, and freefall is an integral part of the adventure. Embrace them, learn from them, and most importantly, enjoy every second of them.

Steering Clear: Navigating the Potholes of Entrepreneurship

Navigating the world of business can sometimes feel like driving on a road full of unexpected potholes. Just when you think you're cruising along smoothly, a challenge appears seemingly out of nowhere, threatening to derail your progress. But much like a seasoned driver anticipates and avoids these roadblocks, a savvy entrepreneur can maneuver around potential pitfalls.

Here's how:

Without Clear Direction, You're Just Drifting: Think of starting a business without a clear vision as driving without a roadmap. It's essential to understand your 'why'. What motivates you? What change are you aiming to bring about? This clarity will serve as your GPS, guiding you towards choices that resonate with your purpose.

Balancing the Books Right: Both splurging at the onset and being overly frugal can lead you into a financial quagmire. Crafting a balanced budget is key. It's less about the amount you allocate and more about making strategic decisions on where your funds go.

The Peril of the One-Man Army: Trying to manage everything single-handedly might feel empowering at first, but it's a surefire route to exhaustion. Recognize where your strengths lie and bring in help for the rest. A cohesive team, whether it's through hiring or outsourcing, can propel your business forward.

Feedback: Your Roadmap to Improvement: Consider your customers as co-navigators on this journey. They'll often spot obstacles or opportunities you might miss. Welcome their feedback and, importantly, don't take it to heart. Use it as a tool to refine and elevate your offerings.

Know When To Change Lanes: Being emotionally tied to an idea or strategy can blind you to better opportunities. Pivoting isn't admitting defeat—it's showcasing your ability to adapt and evolve, hallmarks of a successful entrepreneur.

The "Do I have the mojo?" checklist

Imagine for a moment, you're standing backstage at a talent show. The spotlight awaits, the crowd is buzzing with anticipation, and there's that familiar flutter of excitement mixed with nerves. But there's one vital question hovering in your mind, "Do I have the mojo to wow this crowd?"

Switch back to the entrepreneurial stage. Before you take that leap of faith, before you invest your blood, sweat, and dreams, it's essential to ask: "Do I possess the entrepreneurial mojo?"

It's not just about passion or a brilliant idea. Having the mojo means having the right mix of determination, adaptability, resilience, and a pinch of that unexplainable "it" factor. But how do you quantify this? Fear not, dear reader, for I've distilled decades of experience into this handy checklist. Consider it your roadmap to self-assessment, guiding you towards understanding whether you're truly ready for the limelight.

1. Resilience Radar: Do setbacks fuel your determination rather than diminish it? Can you bounce back with twice the vigor?

2. Curiosity Quotient: Do you have an insatiable appetite for learning? Whether it's market trends, innovations, or understanding what makes your audience tick.

3. Adaptability Adjuster: The business world is ever-evolving. Can you pivot when needed, adapting your strategy on the fly?

4. Visionary Viewfinder: Can you visualize where you want your business to be in 5, 10, or even 20 years?

5. Empathy Engine: Understanding and relating to your customers' needs and pain points is vital. Do you genuinely care about providing solutions that make their lives better?

6. Risk-o-Meter: Are you comfortable with taking calculated risks? Remember, every entrepreneurial journey involves stepping into the unknown.

7. Grit Gauge: When the going gets tough, do you get going? Or are you more likely to throw in the towel?

8. Feedback Filter: Can you take constructive criticism and use it to refine and improve your ideas?

9. Patience Pump: Success rarely happens overnight. Are you in it for the long haul, willing to nurture your venture patiently?

10. Passion Pulse: This one's simple. Do you genuinely love what you're about to embark on?

Now, be brutally honest with yourself. If you find yourself nodding vigorously at most of these points, then my friend, you very likely have the entrepreneurial mojo. But if there are areas where you're unsure or feel lacking, don't be disheartened. Recognize them as growth opportunities, areas where you can seek mentorship or further development.

Because, at the end of the day, having the mojo is about self-awareness, continuous learning, and the burning desire to turn your dream into reality.

Avoiding entrepreneurial burnout: Self-care isn't selfish!

Entrepreneurs, let's have a real heart-to-heart. Do you ever find yourself working late into the night, powered only by caffeine and sheer will? Do days blend into nights, weeks into months, with no pause button in sight? If this rings a bell, welcome to the all-too-familiar world of entrepreneurial burnout. But here's a little wisdom nugget: success, while sweet, loses its flavor when sipped from an empty cup.

Entrepreneurship is a rollercoaster ride of highs, lows, and surprising detours. Within this whirlwind of building dreams, the boundary between passion and overwork can blur, turning drive into exhaustion. Too often, the fiery entrepreneurial spirit, while a force of innovation and determination, becomes its own Achilles' heel when unchecked. Burnout looms when it's all drive and no downtime. Let's delve into the art of avoiding burnout and understand that taking time for yourself isn't indulgence—it's vital for lasting success.

The Signs of a Flame Fading

Burnout isn't a sudden blackout; it's a dimming torch. Some signs to watch out for:

Feeling constantly drained or fatigued
Reduced enthusiasm for a project that once ignited passion
Feelings of cynicism or detachment from work
Reduced productivity or creativity
Difficulty sleeping or chronic restlessness
Refueling Your Torch: Self-Care for the Win!

Pencil It In: Just as you schedule business meetings or project deadlines, mark out "Me Time" in your calendar. Whether it's a 20-minute meditation session, a weekend hike, or simply a coffee break – honor this appointment with yourself.

Delegate, Don't Drown: Remember, entrepreneurship is a marathon, not a sprint. You don't have to do everything yourself. Delegate tasks when possible. Trusting your team can free up mental bandwidth and reduce stress.

Diversify Your Identity: While your business is a significant part of your life, it's not your entirety. Reconnect with hobbies, interests, or communities outside your business sphere. It provides perspective and rejuvenation.

Set Boundaries: Understand that it's okay to say 'no.' Whether it's declining a non-critical meeting after business hours or setting specific 'off-grid' times, setting boundaries can be a game-changer.

Seek Support: Build a support system. Whether it's fellow entrepreneurs, a mentor, or even a therapist specializing in entrepreneurial stress – having someone to share your challenges with can lighten the emotional load.

Self-care isn't a luxury; it's the unsung hero in your success story. So, the next time you feel the flicker of burnout, remember: tending to yourself isn't selfish; it's the fuel that keeps your entrepreneurial torch alight.

Chapter Two

Idea Factory: From Brainstorms to Brain Waves

Idea Excavation: Unearthing Your Business Gold

Starting a business is a lot like being an archaeologist. You're on the hunt, sifting through layers of possibilities, seeking that glimmering artifact that'll define your journey. This process, my fellow entrepreneur-in-the-making, is what I like to call 'Idea Excavation'.

Now, let's get one thing straight. Not every dig will lead you to a treasure. Sometimes, you'll find a broken pot (meaning a flawed idea) or maybe just plain old dirt (an idea that's not quite ripe). And that's perfectly okay! The key is to keep digging, keep exploring, and remain passionate about the quest.

So, how do you go about this excavation? First, arm yourself with the right tools. In the world of business, these tools are your curiosity, market research, and a dash of intuition. Start by asking questions. What does the market need?

What are people complaining about? What's that one thing you wish existed but doesn't?

Next, dig deep. Dive into market trends, study competitors, but more importantly, talk to potential customers. Remember, while gold is valuable, it's often buried deep. The superficial ideas are easy to find, but the golden ones, the ones that lead to success, often require a bit more effort.

The market pulses with its own unique rhythms and patterns. It gives away hints, whispering secrets through reviews, feedback, and social media conversations. Sometimes, the most valuable insights are hidden in the gaps - in what people aren't saying. Perhaps there's a latent demand for an innovative product feature or a niche requirement that's been overlooked by others.

Spotting opportunities is both an art and a science. It's a game of persistence, intuition, and being in the right place at the right time. As you venture through this scavenger hunt, remember, every entrepreneur, from the one-person startup in their garage to the giants of industry, began their journey with a single, potent idea.

And as you dig, don't be disheartened by the occasional rock or obstacle. Every failed attempt, every idea that doesn't pan out, is just a stepping stone, bringing you closer to your golden concept.

Once you've found your potential gold – that brilliant business idea – it's time to polish it. Refine the idea, mold it, shape it, and get ready to present it to the world. But remember, the excavation is just the beginning. Turning that golden idea into a thriving business is where the real adventure lies.

So, to all the budding business archaeologists out there, happy digging! Your golden idea awaits. And once you find it, the journey ahead is going to be one exhilarating ride!

Passion Puzzles: Finding Your Perfect Fit

In the realm of entrepreneurship, aligning your venture with your passion isn't merely a poetic notion—it's also a strategic one. Businesses anchored in genuine interests not only weather challenges more resiliently but also shine brighter during prosperous times. But the question remains: how do you navigate this puzzle of passion?

Set aside business blueprints for a moment and ponder—what ignites your spirit? What topics make you lose track of time in enthusiastic discussion? It could be anything—crafting, tech innovation, storytelling. Identifying this driving force is crucial.

But passion alone isn't the complete picture. Marrying it with your inherent abilities or learned skills is where the magic truly happens. A culinary maestro with a love for global cuisines? An international café might be your calling. A tech aficionado with coding prowess? A software startup could be your next venture.

Delve into communities centered around your passion. Engage, exchange ideas, and absorb feedback. By immersing yourself, you might discover your passion taking new forms influenced by varied viewpoints.

However, while passion is your compass, market viability ensures you're not venturing into a desert. Market research bridges your personal interests with the demands of the real world, ensuring your venture has a receptive audience.

Remember, as you grow, your passions might evolve. Stay receptive to new learnings and enhance your skills. A passion that's continuously refined shines the brightest.

In the entrepreneurial landscape, where many pieces fit together to create the big picture, ensuring your core piece—your passion—is right, is the first step to a fulfilling journey. As you piece together this unique puzzle, let your heart guide you. After all, the most successful ventures aren't just built on strategy and market trends, but on dreams, aspirations, and a fire that refuses to be quenched.

SWOT's Up? Validating Your Golden Idea

Imagine you're about to embark on a grand treasure hunt. You're convinced that X marks the spot and you're about to dig up that golden chest of dreams. But, what if there was a magical map that could hint if you're digging in the right spot? Well, in the entrepreneurial world, we have just that. It's called a SWOT analysis. And no, it's not a fancy new flyswatter!

SWOT stands for Strengths, Weaknesses, Opportunities, and Threats. It's a compass for entrepreneurs, directing both newbies and seasoned vets to validate their business concepts.

Strengths: These are your venture's superpowers! Maybe it's a unique product twist, an exceptional team, or a killer marketing strategy. Recognize them, and don't be humble. This is your time to shine!

Examples:

Personal Passion: Your genuine love for what you do can be infectious and draw customers to you.

Local Knowledge: Understanding your community's needs because you're part of it.

Flexibility: Ability to quickly adapt to customer feedback.

Unique Selling Proposition (USP): What sets your product or service apart? Maybe it's handcrafted goods, or perhaps it's a service provided with personal care.

Weaknesses: Okay, nobody's perfect. These are areas where you might need a bit of buffing and polishing. Is your supply chain a bit rusty? Or maybe your tech isn't up-to-date? Knowing these helps you mend gaps before they turn into pitfalls.

Examples:

Limited Resources: Financial constraints or limited manpower.

Lack of Experience: New to the business and still learning the ropes.

Over-reliance on a few clients: Dependence on a small customer base for the majority of your revenue.

Time Management: Struggling to juggle various roles in the business.

Opportunities: Picture a vast horizon stretched out before you, teeming with possibilities. Maybe there's an emerging market trend that aligns perfectly with your product, or perhaps there's an untapped audience demographic waiting to be discovered. Sail towards these!

Examples:

Growing Community: An increasing number of residents or businesses that can benefit from your offerings.

Unserved Niches: Identifying gaps in the market that larger businesses over-look.

Technology: Utilizing digital platforms to expand your reach or improve service delivery.

Local Events: Collaborating or participating in local events or fairs to increase visibility.

Threats: Think of these as pesky storm clouds on your entrepreneurial journey. It could be a sudden surge in competition, changing regulations, or maybe economic shifts. Being aware means you won't be caught without an umbrella when it rains.

Examples:

Competitors: New businesses opening up, offering similar products/services.

Regulatory Changes: New local regulations or licenses that could impact your operations.

Economic Downturn: Factors that could reduce consumer spending, affecting your business.

Supply Chain Disruptions: Delays in getting essential supplies for your business.

Alright, brave business trailblazer, you've just dipped your toes into the SWOT waters. I've included a SWOT template for you, along with a comprehensive example of a SWOT analysis for a clearer perspective.

Now, it's your turn. Dive into your SWOT grid, methodically filling in each section: Strengths, Weaknesses, Opportunities, and Threats. Delve deep, ensuring every aspect of your business is considered. This isn't just a theoretical exercise; it's a foundational step. The insights you glean might surprise you and prove invaluable. So, before proceeding, I strongly encourage you to complete your SWOT analysis. It's a powerful tool that can unveil actionable insights for your business idea, propelling you forward on your entrepreneurial journey.

Remember, a SWOT analysis isn't a one-and-done task. As your business evolves and the market changes, revisit this guiding map. It'll help keep you in tune with your environment, ensuring that your 'golden idea' remains not only sparkling but also robust.

SWOT ANALYSIS FOR

Green Leaf Café

Date: 11/01/2023

S — Strengths

- **UNIQUE SELLING PROPOSITION (USP)**: GREENLEAF CAFÉ OFFERS ONLY ORGANIC, FAIR-TRADE COFFEE AND LOCALLY-SOURCED PASTRIES
- **LOCATION**: SITUATED IN A BUSTLING PART OF TOWN WITH HIGH FOOT TRAFFIC AND VISIBILITY.
- **SKILLED BARISTAS**: ALL STAFF MEMBERS HAVE UNDERGONE EXTENSIVE TRAINING AND CAN CRAFT A WIDE VARIETY OF COFFEE BEVERAGES.
- **ECO-FRIENDLY BRANDING**: COMMITTED TO SUSTAINABILITY, ALL PACKAGING IS BIODEGRADABLE OR RECYCLABLE, APPEALING TO ENVIRONMENTALLY CONSCIOUS CONSUMERS.

W — Weaknesses

- **LIMITED BRAND RECOGNITION:** AS A NEW ENTRANT IN THE MARKET, GREENLEAF CAFÉ LACKS THE BRAND PRESENCE OF ESTABLISHED COMPETITORS
- **INITIAL COSTS**: HIGH STARTUP EXPENSES DUE TO ORGANIC PRODUCT SOURCING AND ECO-FRIENDLY PACKAGING.
- **LIMITED SEATING CAPACITY**: THE CAFÉ HAS A COZY INTERIOR, BUT SEATING IS LIMITED, WHICH MIGHT DETER LARGER GROUPS.
- **DEPENDENCE ON LOCAL SUPPLIERS**: RELYING HEAVILY ON LOCAL SUPPLIERS CAN LEAD TO POTENTIAL DISRUPTIONS

O — Opportunities

- **GROWING DEMAND FOR ORGANIC PRODUCTS**: A RISING TREND OF CONSUMERS SEEKING ORGANIC AND ECO-FRIENDLY PRODUCTS.
- **LOCAL PARTNERSHIPS**: POTENTIAL TO COLLABORATE WITH LOCAL BUSINESSES FOR JOINT PROMOTIONS OR LOYALTY PROGRAMS.
- **EXPAND PRODUCT LINE**: INTRODUCE NEW ORGANIC TEAS, SNACKS, AND MERCHANDISE TO DIVERSIFY OFFERINGS & INCREASE REVENUE STREAMS.
- **ONLINE PRESENCE**: ESTABLISHING A STRONG ONLINE PRESENCE THROUGH SOCIAL MEDIA MARKETING AND OFFERING ONLINE ORDERS OR DELIVERIES.

T — Threats/Risk

- **COMPETITION**: PRESENCE OF SEVERAL ESTABLISHED COFFEE SHOPS IN THE VICINITY.
- **ECONOMIC DOWNTURN**: ECONOMIC UNCERTAINTIES MIGHT LEAD TO REDUCED CONSUMER SPENDING ON NON-ESSENTIAL ITEMS LIKE SPECIALTY COFFEE.
- **FLUCTUATING COMMODITY PRICES**: PRICES FOR ORGANIC COFFEE BEANS MIGHT INCREASE, AFFECTING PROFIT MARGINS.
- **CHANGING REGULATIONS**: POTENTIAL FOR STRICTER REGULATIONS ON ORGANIC LABELING OR INCREASED TAXES ON SMALL BUSINESSES.

SWOT ANALYSIS FOR

Date : _______________

S
Strengths

W
Weaknesses

O
Opportunities

T
Threats/Risk

SWOT ANALYSIS FOR

Date : _______________

S
Strengths

W
Weaknesses

O
Opportunities

T
Threats/Risk

SWOT ANALYSIS FOR

Date : _______________

S — Strengths

W — Weaknesses

O — Opportunities

T — Threats/Risk

Chapter Three

Navigating the Business Seas: Red Sharks or Blue Whales

Red or Blue? Choosing Your Oceanic Adventure

Picture yourself standing at the helm of a ship. The salty sea breeze is ruffling your hair, and the vast expanse of ocean stretches out before you. Two distinct paths emerge in the distance: one teeming with aggressive, fast-moving red sharks and another inhabited by massive, serene blue whales. This isn't a dream, nor is it a sci-fi flick. This, my dear entrepreneur, is a decision every business owner faces: the choice between the Red Ocean and the Blue Ocean strategy.

Now, before you start imagining Jaws-esque scenarios, let's debunk this maritime myth.

Red Ocean Strategy: Think of this as the bloody waters of fierce competition. It's where businesses fight tooth and nail over a pre-existing market space, trying to outperform their rivals and snatch a larger piece of the existing market pie. It's all about beating the competition. Sounds intense? It is!

Examples:

Coke vs. Pepsi: These beverage giants have been battling for market dominance for decades, continuously trying to outdo each other with marketing campaigns, new product variations, and more.

Nike vs. Adidas: In the athletic footwear and apparel sector, these two brands are in a continuous rivalry, launching new product lines, endorsements, and marketing campaigns to gain a larger market share.

Pros:

Established market with known demand.

Clear competitive benchmarks.

Cons:

Margins often get squeezed due to competition.

Requires continuous innovation to stay ahead.

Blue Ocean Strategy: Here, instead of waging war in overcrowded waters, businesses explore uncharted territories. They create new market spaces or "Blue Oceans", making competition irrelevant. It's all about innovation and creating a new market, rather than fighting over an existing one.

Examples:

Cirque du Soleil: By reimagining the traditional circus, Cirque du Soleil blended theater and circus arts, creating an entirely new market in the entertainment industry.

Nintendo's Wii: Instead of competing head-to-head with powerful gaming consoles, Nintendo introduced the Wii, targeting casual gamers and families, thereby creating a new market segment.

Pros:

Opportunity to set the rules of the game.

Often results in higher profit margins as there's no competition (yet).

Cons:

Venturing into uncharted territories; there's a chance your unique offering might not resonate with a sizable market.

Navigating the uncertainty of whether there's genuine demand for your novel idea.

Requires a deeper understanding of potential customer needs.

So, which oceanic path should you choose? It's a bit like deciding between playing it safe on familiar shores or charting a course into the unknown in search of undiscovered islands. Each strategy has its merits, and the right one for you will depend on your risk tolerance, resources, and the unique value you bring to the table.

Remember, while the Red Ocean is bustling and can feel like an adrenaline-packed gladiator match, the Blue Ocean offers the allure of serene waters and the potential for unparalleled success. But it also comes with its challenges. Just like with any great voyage, preparation and understanding of the seas (or strategies) you're entering will be your greatest allies.

The Dual Strategy: Exploring Both Oceans

While the Red and Blue Oceans present distinct strategies, they are not mutually exclusive. Sometimes, the best route forward is a combination of both. As an entrepreneur, you might find yourself oscillating between these waters or even merging the two strategies to craft your unique path.

Bridging the Gap: The Grey Ocean Strategy

Imagine a spectrum where the bloody red waters start to merge with the deep blue seas, creating a vast, swirling expanse of grey. This is the Grey Ocean Strategy, a hybrid approach that combines the best of both worlds.

Pros:

Flexibility: You're not confined to just one strategy. You can pivot between aggressive competition and innovative exploration based on market dynamics.

Balanced Risk: While you might not enjoy the high profit margins of a purely Blue Ocean Strategy, you also won't be exposed to its high uncertainty.

Diverse Revenue Streams: Operating in both oceans allows you to tap into established markets while also seeking out new opportunities.

Cons:

Resource Allocation: Juggling between two strategies might stretch your resources, requiring a delicate balancing act.

Potential Identity Crisis: There's a risk that your brand might get diluted if you're trying to be everything to everyone.

Case in Point: Hybrid Successes
Take the case of Apple. While they revolutionized the tech industry with their innovative products, creating a Blue Ocean with the iPod, iPhone, and iPad, they also fiercely compete in the saturated smartphone and computer markets, a classic Red Ocean.

Or consider the rise of hybrid cars. Companies like Toyota didn't just compete with other car manufacturers in terms of efficiency and price (Red Ocean). They also introduced an entirely new concept to the market with the Prius, creating a Blue Ocean of environmentally conscious consumers.

In Conclusion: Charting Your Unique Course

As you stand at your business's helm, know that the ocean you choose doesn't confine you. The seas of business strategy are vast and interconnected. You can start in the Red Ocean, gain expertise and resources, and then venture into the Blue, or vice versa. And if you're feeling particularly adventurous, you can dive into the Grey Ocean, merging the strategies to create a unique splash in the market.

Your journey is yours to define. So, with a clear vision, a steady hand, and the wind in your sails, set forth and conquer whichever ocean calls out to you!

Chapter Four

Fear Busters: Overcoming Entrepreneurial Anxieties

Breaking the Chains of Doubt

You know the feeling: that little voice in the back of your head whispering "Are you sure?" or "What if you fail?" Doubt is like the rust that threatens to weaken and corrode even the strongest of metals. But before we dive into our toolkit to combat this pesky ghost, let's first understand it.

Doubt is natural, and honestly, it's healthy in doses. It makes us question, review, and refine our strategies. However, when left unchecked, doubt can paralyze, causing inaction or making us abandon ship even before we've left the harbor.

It's heartening to remember that every entrepreneur, from the likes of Steve Jobs to Oprah Winfrey, has grappled with this very issue. Experiencing doubt isn't an indictment of your capabilities; rather, it's an intrinsic part of the entrepreneurial odyssey.

Suppressing these feelings only offers fertile ground for doubt to thrive. Open up about it. Seek counsel from trusted mentors, friends, or peers. Often, voicing these apprehensions can lend clarity, transforming nebulous fears into tangible challenges to overcome.

Much of our doubt stems from the unnerving vastness of the unknown. One of the most potent weapons against it is knowledge. Delve into research, partake in courses, immerse in workshops. Familiarizing yourself with the intricacies of your domain can banish many uncertainties.

Yet, at times, action is the most eloquent response to doubt. Begin with incremental steps, gauge the terrain, and savor each stride forward as a testament to your resilience against apprehension.

Inhale deeply, and let the invigorating air of conviction fill you. This is merely the dawn of your odyssey. While doubt is an inevitable phantom in the entrepreneurial night, armed with determination, knowledge, and courage, your narrative will resound more with tales of triumph than of tribulations.

Balancing on the Tightrope: Risk, Fall, and Getting Back Up

The entrepreneurial journey isn't a straight paved road—it's more like a tightrope suspended over the vast expanse of the unknown. One moment, you're on cloud nine, celebrating a victory, and the next, you're grappling with an unforeseen challenge. It's an exhilarating, daunting, and profoundly rewarding balancing act.

Before setting out, it's essential to understand the nature of this journey. Just as a tightrope is narrow and unstable, entrepreneurship offers no guarantees. Winds of challenge will attempt to throw you off balance, but being mentally prepared ensures you're not easily shaken.

Much like no tightrope walker would venture without their safety harness, you shouldn't step into the business world without your safeguards: comprehensive knowledge, a robust plan, and a dependable team. These tools don't promise a falter-free journey, but they ensure that when you wobble—and you will—you have the means to regain your footing swiftly.

Even with the best preparations, missteps are inevitable. Whether it's due to unforeseen market shifts, personal challenges, or other unexpected events, it's essential to remember that these wobbles are not failures—they're tests of resilience and adaptability. Embrace them, learn from them, and use the experience to fortify your approach.

And, on the off chance that you do fall, whether from a failed product launch or a financial oversight, know that the heart of entrepreneurship lies not in the fall, but in the recovery. It's how you rise, reflect, recalibrate, and relaunch that truly defines your journey. After all, the most memorable tales from successful entrepreneurs often revolve around monumental comebacks after setbacks.

Lastly, remember that this tightrope journey doesn't have to be a solitary one. The entrepreneurial community is rich with mentors and peers whose experiences and guidance can serve as invaluable support. Engaging in simple conversations over coffee or brainstorming sessions can reinvigorate your spirit, offering fresh perspectives and renewed confidence.

Walking the entrepreneurial tightrope is not for the faint of heart. But oh, the views from up here! The sheer thrill of crafting your path, the exhilaration of conquering challenges, and the unmatched joy of seeing your vision turn into reality. So, chin up, deep breath, and step forward. Each stride you take on this adventure takes you closer to your dreams.

Confidence Cocktails: Mixing the Perfect Blend

Imagine standing at a chic bar, the ambient lighting creating a warm glow, and you're handed a menu filled with vibrant cocktails. Each drink is a mixture of distinct ingredients that, when blended right, create magic. Similarly, in the business realm, confidence isn't just a one-note trait. It's a concoction of self-belief, experience, and positive affirmations. Let's play bartender for a bit, shall we? Here's your guide to mixing the perfect 'confidence cocktail.'

Start With a Base of Self-Awareness

Like a good old gin or vodka, self-awareness is the base of your cocktail. It's about recognizing your strengths and acknowledging your weak spots. This is not to dwell on them but to improve, adapt, and grow. Being aware of where you stand sets a realistic platform from which you can leap confidently.

Add a Splash of Positive Affirmation

Think of positive affirmations as that zesty splash of lime or tonic, elevating your drink. Daily reminders of your capabilities, past successes, and potential can change your mindset. It shifts focus from 'I can't' to 'How can I?' Remember, the narrative you tell yourself daily molds your reality.

Stir in Experience

Like a bartender mastering his craft with each drink he stirs, every experience, be it a win or loss, shapes your confidence. Embrace all experiences, learn from your missteps, and cherish your wins. The more you immerse yourself in the world of entrepreneurship, the richer your confidence cocktail becomes.

Garnish with Feedback

Feedback is your garnish – the finishing touch. Whether it's from mentors, peers, or customers, feedback provides clarity. It tells you what's working and what needs tweaking. And while not all feedback is easy to swallow, it's crucial for growth and solidifying your confidence.

Sip, Don't Chug

Rushing confidence is like downing a cocktail. It might give a quick high but can also lead to a steep crash. True confidence is savored, built sip by sip, with each challenge faced, every hurdle crossed, and lessons learned along the way.

Keep Experimenting

Lastly, remember that the perfect blend is subjective. What works for one might not work for another. So, don't hesitate to revisit and adjust your ingredients. Entrepreneurship, after all, is about evolving, and so is the art of confidence-building.

Cheers to you and your ever-evolving blend of self-assurance! With the right mix of elements, your confidence cocktail will not only be the star of your entrepreneurial bar but also the secret sauce to tackling any challenge that comes your way. So, the next time self-doubt tries to crash your party, raise your glass high and sip on your meticulously crafted confidence.

Overcoming Limiting Beliefs with Dr. Albert Ellis's ABC Model

Navigating the entrepreneurial journey, we frequently encounter hurdles. Yet, it's often not external barriers but our internal convictions that tether us down. Dr. Albert Ellis, a renowned psychologist, pioneered a model to identify and challenge these often irrational beliefs that hinder us. Let's unpack this.

The ABCs of Your Beliefs:

A for Activating Event: This is the situation or event that triggers a thought or emotional response. For entrepreneurs, this could be anything from receiving a negative product review to facing financial challenges.

B for Belief: Following the activating event, we form a belief about the situation. This belief might be rational (based on facts or reality) or irrational (based on assumptions, biases, or past experiences).

C for Consequence: This is the emotional or behavioral response resulting from our belief.

Identifying Irrational Beliefs in Entrepreneurship:

Let's take a real-world example.

A (Activating Event): A potential investor decides not to fund your startup.

B (Belief): "I always mess up. No one believes in my vision. Maybe I'm not cut out for this."

C (Consequence): You feel disheartened, consider giving up, or shy away from approaching other potential investors.

Challenging the Belief:

The key lies in identifying the 'B'—the belief—and challenging its authenticity. Are you really always messing up, or have there been moments of success? Is it truly that no one believes in your vision, or is it just that this particular investor's priorities didn't align with yours?

By dissecting the belief, you often find that it's based on exaggerations, generalizations, or black-and-white thinking.

Transforming the Belief:

Once identified, transform the irrational belief into a more balanced and rational one. Instead of "I always mess up," consider the belief, "I've faced setbacks before and overcome them. This is another challenge to navigate."

With the revised belief, the consequence then becomes more positive. You might feel momentarily disappointed but remain resilient and approach other potential investors with renewed vigor.

In the unpredictable realm of entrepreneurship, setbacks are inevitable. Yet, with Dr. Ellis's ABC Model, you equip yourself with a robust tool to ensure that your internal beliefs don't amplify these challenges. Instead of being trapped in self-defeating cycles, you can swiftly identify, challenge, and transform these beliefs, forging ahead with clarity and confidence.

Part II: The Business Basecamp: Establishing the Foundation

Chapter Five

Cashing in on Your Dream: Pathways of Business Funding

Bootstrapping: Rolling Up Your Sleeves

Dive into the entrepreneurial world, and you'll likely hear whispers of "bootstrapping." It's not about fancy footwear but is one of the fundamental steps for many fledgling businesses. Bootstrapping simply means funding your business using your own resources, be it savings, reinvested profits, or personal credit. It's the financial equivalent of rolling up your sleeves and saying, "I've got this!"

But why would anyone choose bootstrapping, especially when there are other enticing funding avenues available? First, it offers complete control. No external investors mean no one else calling the shots. You remain the captain of your ship, charting your course without outside interference.

Furthermore, bootstrapping instills a sense of discipline. When it's your hard-earned money on the line, you tend to make more calculated, conscientious decisions. Every penny counts, and this awareness can lead to a leaner, more efficient business model.

Now, while the benefits are clear, it's essential to be cautious. Pouring all your savings into your dream venture sounds romantic, but real life isn't always a fairy tale. It's crucial to strike a balance, ensuring you don't jeopardize your personal financial security. Always keep a safety net—funds to cover personal expenses and emergencies.

If you decide to go down the bootstrapping route, here are some golden nuggets:

Start Small and Scale Gradually: Begin with a minimum viable product (MVP) and expand as you gain traction. It reduces initial costs and allows you to test the waters.

Keep Overheads Low: Opt for co-working spaces, use open-source software, and, if feasible, start your venture from home.

Reinvest Profits: Instead of splurging on luxuries, pour the profits back into the business to fuel growth.

Stay Frugal, Not Stingy: Recognize the difference between essential and non-essential expenses. Invest where it counts but don't be overly extravagant.

In essence, bootstrapping is like planting a seed and nurturing it with care, patience, and dedication. It may not offer the instant gratification of a big investor check, but it gives something more profound: a sense of accomplishment and the joy of seeing your brainchild grow organically. And who knows? With the right moves and a sprinkle of luck, you might just turn those pennies in a jar into a flourishing empire.

Crowdfunding: Rallying the Troops for Your Vision

Step into the bustling bazaar of the digital age, and you'll find a corner brimming with dreamers, innovators, and their chorus of supporters. This is crowdfunding, where concepts transform into tangible realities backed by the collective power of the community.

Kickstarter and Indiegogo are the big players of this universe, platforms where individuals pledge money to projects they believe in. Think of them as a stage, where you, the creator, pitch your dream to an audience eager to be part of the next big thing.

Kickstarter operates on an all-or-nothing principle. You set a financial goal and a deadline. If you hit the target by the due date, hooray, the funds are yours! If not, the pledges are returned to the backers, leaving you with valuable feedback and perhaps another shot at the drawing board.

Indiegogo, while similar to Kickstarter in many aspects, offers more flexibility. They have a 'Flexible Funding' option where you keep the raised funds, even if you don't meet the set goal. However, remember, with greater flexibility comes a slightly higher fee.

Now, merely having a platform isn't enough. It's the story you tell, the passion you exude, and the vision you share that truly makes the difference. So, how do you craft a campaign that not only attracts eyes but also opens wallets?

Be genuine. Share your story, your journey, and the reason behind your project. People resonate with realness.

Ensure your project's essence is communicated succinctly. Your audience should grasp the what, why, and how within the first few moments.

An engaging video can exponentially boost your campaign's appeal. Keep it professional, crisp, and, most importantly, heartwarming.

Offer backers rewards that are both valuable and unique. Whether it's a limited-edition product, a behind-the-scenes tour, or even a simple thank-you note, make them feel special.

Keep your backers in the loop. Share progress, challenges, milestones, and gratitude. Make them feel they're on this journey with you.

Use social media, email campaigns, and even good ol' word-of-mouth. The more visibility your campaign gets, the higher the chances of reaching your goal.

Crowdfunding isn't just about raising funds; it's about building a community around your idea. It's the thrill of seeing complete strangers turn into ardent supporters, all because they believe in your dream. Gear up, put your best foot forward, and remember: the world is brimming with potential backers just waiting to be inspired by a vision like yours!

Angel Investors and Venture Capitalists

Navigating the world of startup financing can sometimes feel overwhelming Two key players in this realm are Angel Investors and Venture Capitalists, and while they both fund startups, their approaches and interests are distinct.

Angel Investors are individuals who, seeing potential in your entrepreneurial aspirations, decide to back you. They have a surplus in funds and a keen eye for budding talent. Often, they invest in startups, usually in exchange for equity. Their hallmark? They're more than just financiers. They offer mentorship, wisdom, and insights from their experiences. Their engagement with small businesses often goes beyond money, extending to genuine advice and guidance.

Venture Capitalists (VCs), on the other hand, are the big leagues of start-up funding. These are professional entities, aggregating and managing funds from various investors, directing them toward startups that showcase significant promise. VCs typically enter the scene when your venture has matured beyond the initial phase, signaling a product or even an existing customer base. They bring in substantial investments, but with that comes heightened expectations. Their primary goal? They're hunting for ventures that promise exponential growth and substantial returns.

However, a crucial distinction for startups, especially small businesses, is recognizing that VC funding might not always be the best avenue. VCs prioritize scalability and explosive growth, focusing on high returns. A local business with modest growth aspirations might not align with a VC's objectives. Securing VC funding can also introduce pressures to scale rapidly, which might not resonate with every entrepreneur's vision or business model.

So, how does one attract these financial stalwarts?

For Angel Investors, it's often about personal connection and trust. They're investing in the person as much as the idea. It's essential to display passion, commitment, and transparency about both the potential and the pitfalls of the venture.

For VCs, it's paramount to underscore scalability and demonstrate a trajectory of rapid growth. Robust data, clear market potential, and a cohesive, skilled team can tilt the scales in your favor.

Bank Loans and Credit Lines

Dive into your comfiest chair, brew a cuppa, and let's journey into the often mysterious, occasionally intimidating, but surprisingly approachable world of bank loans and credit lines. If you ever thought of banks as stuffy institutions with towering pillars, it's time to view them as potential allies in your entrepreneurial quest. With the right preparation and a sprinkle of charm, they might just become your startup's fairy godmother.

First on our radar is understanding the types of bank loans tailored for businesses like yours. It's akin to a wardrobe - different outfits for different occasions!

Term Loans: Think of these as your business' little black dress or well-fitted suit. They're classic. You borrow a lump sum and repay it, with interest, over a fixed period. These are ideal for hefty one-time expenses like acquiring new equipment or expanding to a new location.

Lines of Credit: These are your versatile pair of jeans – reliable, flexible, and always there when you need them. Instead of a lump sum, you're given access to a pool of funds which you can dip into as needed, only paying interest on what you use. Perfect for managing cash flow or unexpected expenses.

Equipment Financing: The flashy sneakers of the loan world. This is specifically for purchasing equipment. The equipment itself serves as collateral, making it easier to secure.

Commercial Real Estate Loans: The chic, sleek business coat. Intended for buying property for your business operations. It's a big commitment but can be a game-changer for businesses looking to establish a permanent base.

With the types down, let's prep for that bank date. You don't want to walk in blind, do you?

Business Plan: It's like your resume. A well-drafted business plan tells your bank that you mean well... business. It showcases your understanding of the market, financial projections, and the strategies in place.

Credit Score: The equivalent of your reputation in high school. A high score indicates you're responsible with money, making banks more likely to lend.

Financial Statements: Your report cards, essentially. Balance sheets, profit-loss statements – they offer a snapshot of your business's financial health.

Collateral: Sometimes, banks want a safety net. This could be in the form of equipment, property, or other assets that the bank can claim if you can't repay.

Understanding Terms: Before signing on the dotted line, ensure you understand the interest rates, any associated fees, and the repayment schedule. It's like reading the rules before a game – it just makes everything smoother.

Navigating the world of bank loans and credit lines might seem daunting, but remember, banks want to lend to promising businesses. It's their bread and butter. Your job? Present your venture as a tantalizing slice of the business pie, ripe for the taking. Armed with knowledge, preparation, and a dash of confidence, you're all set to make the bank an offer they can't refuse!

Grants and Business Competitions

Grants are essentially the business world's scholarships. These are non-repayable funds provided by one party (often governmental bodies, foundations, or corporations) to a recipient, typically a business, nonprofit organization, or an individual. The primary catch? No, you're not selling a kidney! Instead, you're often expected to use these funds for a specific purpose, like research, business expansion, or community projects. The allure of grants is undeniable: free money to fuel your entrepreneurial dreams. But, and it's a 'but' worth noting, they often come with strings attached. Think of them like a gift card, reserved for particular spending.

Where can one find these elusive grants? Government websites are treasure troves, often listing available grants and their prerequisites. Foundations and corporations with a CSR (Corporate Social Responsibility) arm also offer grants that align with their mission. There are also specialized directories and platforms that consolidate grant opportunities for ease of access.

Now, let's switch gears to business competitions. If you've ever watched "Shark Tank", you've gotten a glimpse into the world of competitive business pitching. It's not just about winning an investment. These platforms are high-energy arenas where entrepreneurs get to spotlight their ideas, get invaluable feedback, and network with industry stalwarts. Winning is fantastic, of course, but the feedback, exposure, and contacts you make are equally golden.

When stepping into a competition, it's essential to have a pitch that's compelling and crisp. Define your unique selling proposition, highlight the problem you're solving, and showcase the potential for growth and impact.

Chapter Six

Mastering Money: Finance & Tax 101

Fundamentals of Financial Mastery

Navigating the financial landscape of your business might seem daunting at first, but by understanding a few key elements, you can gain clarity and confidence.

Start with the Income Statement. This document provides a detailed look at your business's performance over a specific period. It lists your revenues (the money coming in) against your expenses (the money going out). By comparing these two, you can determine if your business is profitable. A positive difference indicates profit, while a negative one suggests a loss. Regularly reviewing this statement helps identify trends and make informed financial decisions.

Next in line is the Balance Sheet. It's a snapshot of your business's financial position at a specific point in time. It categorizes your assets (everything your business owns) and your liabilities (everything your business owes). The difference between assets and liabilities gives your equity, which represents your ownership value in the business. A healthy balance sheet is foundational for any business's financial stability.

Then, we have the Cash Flow Statement. It tracks how money moves in and out of your business. This document is vital for understanding your operational efficiency and ensuring there's always enough cash on hand to cover expenses.

Expense Management is another vital area. By keeping a keen eye on your expenses, you can identify opportunities for savings and make strategic investment decisions. It's not just about tracking but understanding the "why" behind each expense.

It's also crucial to maintain Reserves. These are funds set aside for unexpected expenses. In business, unforeseen costs can arise, and having a reserve ensures you can handle them without compromising your operations.

Lastly, understanding your Profit Margins is essential. This metric helps you gauge the profitability of each sale. Monitoring and analyzing profit margins can offer insights into pricing strategies and operational efficiencies.

Mastering these elements is more than just crunching numbers. It's about gaining insights into the health and potential of your business. With a solid understanding of these financial principles, you're well-equipped to steer your business toward success.

Budgeting: The Financial Blueprint

Creating a budget isn't about restricting your ambitions but guiding them. Start with listing all anticipated sources of income – be it sales, investments, or other revenue streams. Once you've pinned down your incoming funds, it's time to dissect your expected expenses. We're talking the biggies, like rent and salaries, but also those sneaky smaller costs like monthly software subscriptions or the occasional office coffee run.

And remember, the beauty of budgeting lies in its dynamism. It's not about chiseling numbers in stone; it's about sculpting them in clay, allowing for tweaks and adjustments. The world of business is as unpredictable as it is exciting. Say a product is selling like hotcakes – awesome! You might need to pivot your budget to support increased production. Conversely, if an advertising strategy is a dud, redirect that budget segment elsewhere.

Regularly revisiting your budget ensures that you're not just keeping track of your financial pulse but also adapting to the business's ever-changing rhythm. It's all about flexibility and ensuring every penny has a purpose.

In wrapping up our budget chat, remember this: it's more than just numbers on a spreadsheet. It's a roadmap, a compass, a strategic game plan. Embrace the art of budgeting, and it will undoubtedly steer your business venture toward success.

Financial Forecasting: Charting Your Business's Future

Ahoy, entrepreneur! Just as a seasoned sailor relies on star maps and compasses to navigate the vast seas, your business requires financial forecasting to chart its course in the expansive world of commerce. Financial forecasting is less about crystal balls and more about informed predictions. It's the art and science of anticipating future financial trends based on past and present data.

Begin your forecasting journey by understanding your revenue streams. What are the patterns? Are there seasonal spikes or dips? By analyzing these trends, you can anticipate when cash will flow into your coffers. But remember, the seas of business are unpredictable. While past data is a valuable compass, stay alert to changing winds and currents, like market shifts or global economic trends.

On the flip side, forecasting isn't just about revenue. It's equally crucial to predict your future expenses. From fixed costs like rent to variable ones like marketing campaigns, having a clear projection helps ensure you're never caught off guard.

One essential element of forecasting is scenario planning. Think of it as having different maps for various sea conditions. Create a conservative estimate where things remain steady, an optimistic one where your business sails with favorable winds, and a pessimistic scenario where you might face a few storms. This approach ensures you're prepared for calm seas and rough waters alike.

Lastly, treat your forecast as a living document. Regularly update it with actual financial results and adjust your course as needed. In the vast ocean of business, conditions change, and a flexible approach ensures you remain on the right path.

Incorporate this financial compass into your journey, and you'll find it easier to steer towards uncharted territories, discover new islands of opportunity, and avoid potential icebergs.

Financial Metrics and Indicators

So, you've familiarized yourself with basic financial statements, crafted a robust budget and a financial forecast. It's time to delve deeper into the fascinating world of financial metrics and indicators. These are the tools that'll give you a crystal-clear view of your business's financial pulse.

KPIs, or Key Performance Indicators, are like the vital signs you'd see on a medical chart, except they gauge the health of your business. They help you identify strengths, weaknesses, and areas of improvement, ensuring you stay on track and pivot when necessary.

Profitability Ratios are essentially your business's report card. They tell you how much profit you're making relative to your sales or investments. A great profitability ratio? A gold star. But if they're a tad lackluster, it's time to investigate further.

Liquidity Ratios, on the other hand, are about readiness. Can you meet short-term financial obligations? A solid liquidity ratio indicates you're poised to handle the ebb and flow of expenses.

But let's dig deeper. Here are some universal KPIs that many businesses, regardless of their niche, can benefit from tracking:

Break-even Point: This informs you of how many units or what amount of service you must sell to cover costs.

Gross Margin: A percentage that tells you how much of your sales revenue is profit after subtracting the cost of goods sold.

Net Profit Margin: Reveals the percentage of revenue left after all expenses are deducted from sales.

Customer Retention Rate: This number tells you how good you are at keeping customers coming back for more.

Revenue Growth Rate: Shows how quickly your business's revenue is growing.

Mastering the Tax Terrain: Business Essentials and Deductions

We're diving into everyone's "favorite" topic: taxes! Okay, I hear you. Tax isn't the sexiest subject in the entrepreneurial universe, but it's undeniably crucial. And who knows? With the right information and attitude, you might just start seeing taxes in a more favorable light.

First off, there's a silver lining to the tax cloud: deductions. When it comes to business, you'll find a variety of potential deductions waiting to be claimed. Things like office supplies, travel expenses, or even a portion of your home if you're using it as a workspace. Basically, expenses that are essential for running your business could be deductible, meaning they reduce the amount of income you're taxed on. Now, doesn't that sound a tad more appealing?

However, and this is a big 'however,' it's paramount to ensure you're not just randomly claiming deductions. It's all about being accurate and truthful. Exaggerating or misreporting can lead to hefty penalties and a lot of unnecessary stress. So, it's essential to familiarize yourself with what's allowed in your specific business realm.

Then comes the all-important task of timely tax filings. Procrastination might be fine for choosing your weekend plans, but with taxes, it's a no-go. Late filings can mean penalties, interest, and a potential audit flag. Let's face it; nobody wants the tax authorities knocking on their door. So, mark your calendar, set reminders, and maybe even sprinkle some glitter on the date – whatever it takes to ensure you file on time.

Proper record-keeping is the unsung hero of tax season. Think of it as the backstage crew at a concert; you might not see them, but boy, do they make the show possible! Keeping meticulous records of your expenses, incomes, and any potential deductions not only eases your tax filing process but it also ensures you're prepared if any questions arise. Plus, it's a tremendous help in understanding your financial health.

Wrapping up our tax tour, I want to emphasize that while it's essential to be informed and proactive about your taxes, it's equally crucial to consider seeking expertise when needed. A good accountant or tax professional can be an invaluable ally, guiding you through the maze and ensuring you're making the most of your financial situation. Taxes might never become your favorite topic, but with the right approach, they don't have to be your nemesis either. Happy filing!

Chapter Seven

Blueprint for Success: Crafting Your Business Plan

Introduction

In the realm of business, a solid foundation is everything. Much like the architect who needs a detailed blueprint to construct a towering skyscraper, the astute entrepreneur can greatly benefit from a well-crafted business plan. It serves as a strategic guide, offering clarity and direction for your venture as it grows and evolves.

However, in an ever-changing entrepreneurial landscape, traditional norms are frequently challenged. For instance, within tech circles and innovative start-ups, a sleek PowerPoint presentation often replaces the comprehensive business plan during pitches. It's essential to recognize that while valuable, a conventional business plan isn't universally mandatory.

But before you opt out and bypass this step, it's worth understanding its intrinsic value. A business plan, beyond providing a roadmap, often acts as a touchstone—offering insights during times of uncertainty and helping anchor decisions that align with core objectives.

If you're targeting conventional funding avenues or striving for a rigorous, in-depth strategy to safeguard your vision, the merits of a business plan are undeniable. However, the ultimate choice is yours. Whether you embrace this tool or seek alternative methods, the key is to stay true to your venture's unique needs and aspirations.

For those poised to venture into the intricate yet immensely rewarding domain of business plan creation, this chapter aims to be a comprehensive guide. Together, let's explore the components that can set the stage for your business's continued success.

Ingredients for a Sizzling Business Plan

Think of your business plan as a gourmet dish. To whip up a culinary masterpiece, every chef knows the importance of quality ingredients. Similarly, the efficacy of your business plan hinges on integrating vital components that resonate with your goals, audience, and vision.

You wouldn't expect a cake to rise without the leavening agent, nor a soup to dazzle without the right seasoning. In the world of business, missing a core element can make your plan feel lackluster or incomplete. But fear not! We're about to embark on a culinary journey of sorts—one where we unpack the essential ingredients that can elevate your business plan from good to absolutely delicious.

From the zest of a clear vision to the robustness of accurate financials, each component plays a role. And just like in cooking, it's not only about having the right ingredients but also about how you blend them together.

Ready to don your entrepreneurial chef's hat? Let's dive into the recipe for a sizzling business plan that is bound to tantalize investors and give clarity to your business trajectory.

Executive Summary

Purpose: Often read first but written last, this is a snapshot of your business as a whole. It sets the tone and makes the case for why your business matters.

Key Components: Introduction to your business, your mission statement, and an overview of products or services. Give a brief account of the company's history and its plans for the future.

Business Description

Purpose: To provide an in-depth look at your business, allowing readers to understand the specific nuances of your industry.

Key Components: Description of the industry's current status and future outlook. Detailed information about your business, its goals, and how it will address market needs.

Market Analysis

Purpose: To showcase your knowledge about the specific market segment you're targeting.

Key Components: Detailed descriptions of your target customer segment, including demographics and behavior patterns. Analysis of your competitors, highlighting their strengths and weaknesses. Showcase market trends, predict future growth, and identify potential challenges.

Organization and Management

Purpose: To present your business's organizational structure.

Key Components: Detailed company hierarchy, profiles of your management team, their roles, and their relevant experience. Include an organizational chart if applicable.

Service or Product Line

Purpose: To offer a detailed view of what you're selling or what service you're offering.

Key Components: Descriptions of products or services, their lifecycle, and any R&D activities. Highlight benefits to the consumer and potential product evolution.

Sales and Marketing

Purpose: To outline how you'll bring your product to market and attract and retain customers.

Key Components: Break down your sales strategy, marketing and advertising strategies, pricing strategy, and distribution channels. Explain how you'll maintain customer engagement and loyalty.

Funding Request

Purpose: Essential if you're seeking financial support.

Key Components: Clearly specify the amount of funding required, its use (be it for capital expenditure, operational costs, or expansion activities), and the type of funding you're requesting.

Financial Projections

Purpose: To persuade investors that your business is stable and will be profitable.

Key Components: Include income statements, balance sheets, cash flow statements, and capital expenditure budgets. If possible, provide a financial outlook for the next five years.

Appendix

Purpose: To provide additional resources or references that could bolster your plan.

Key Components: Any supporting documents such as resumes, permits, leases, contracts, and other pertinent information.

While these are the foundational ingredients, remember that every business plan is as unique as the entrepreneur behind it. Depending on your business type, industry, and target audience, you might need to add more sections or elaborate further on specific parts.

Now, with these ingredients in hand, you're set to stir, blend, and whisk your way to a flavorful and effective business plan!

Serving it hot: Presenting with pizzazz

So, you've got your meticulously crafted business plan in hand, layered with details like a gourmet lasagna. But here's the secret sauce: it's not just what you present, it's how you present it. Even the most captivating story can lose its allure if narrated in a monotone. As our quest in the entrepreneurial realm continues, it's time to sprinkle some pizzazz on our presentation.

Know Your Audience: Before you even begin, understand who you're speaking to. An investor might need financials up front, while a potential partner may be more interested in the operational details. Tailor your presentation to captivate their interests.

Storytelling is Key: Your business plan isn't a cold list of facts. It's your business story, filled with passion, challenges, and aspirations. Narrate it, don't just read it.

Visuals, Visuals, Visuals: Humans are visual creatures. Spice up your presentation with engaging graphics, charts, and images. This isn't about making it "pretty" but making complex data easily digestible.

Practice Makes Perfect: No matter how well-acquainted you are with your business, practice your presentation. Get the timing right, polish those transitions, and ensure you're fluent in every aspect.

Engage, Don't Monologue: Encourage questions. Make it a conversation, not a one-sided monologue. This not only keeps your audience engaged but also shows that you're open to feedback.

Confidence is Your Superpower: Believe in what you're presenting. Your confidence will lend credibility to your words and instill trust in your audience.

Provide Takeaways: At the end of your presentation, provide handouts or digital summaries. This ensures your key points remain with your audience long after the presentation concludes.

Adapt on the Fly: Sometimes, despite all preparations, you'll face curveballs – unexpected questions, tech glitches, or changes in the audience's mood. Be ready to adapt, pivot, and improvise.

Finish Strong: Conclude with a call to action or a powerful closing statement that reinforces your main message. Leave your audience with something to ponder, discuss, or act upon.

While your business plan is the main course, your presentation style is the seasoning. Without the right balance, even the most flavorful dish can taste bland. Whether you're presenting to a room full of potential investors, a single potential partner, or a community forum, serve your business plan hot, seasoned with flair, and watch your audience savor every bite!

Chapter Eight

Decoding the Legal Jungle

Your Business Kingdom: Choosing the Right Business Structure

Think of your new business venture as a majestic castle, a testament to your dreams, passion, and hard work. But before you hoist the flag or let down the drawbridge, you've got to lay that very first stone: the foundation of your business, or more precisely, its legal structure.

Now, I get it. Legal mumbo-jumbo isn't everyone's cup of tea (or goblet of wine, in our castle metaphor), but it's essential to get this part right. You see, your business's structure influences nearly every aspect of your enterprise, from how much you pay in taxes to your personal liability. So, let's dive in, and I promise, we'll make it as thrilling as a knight's tournament!

Sole Proprietorships: Going Solo in the Business World

Ah, the lone wolf approach. The solitary ruler of your realm.

As the name suggests, a sole proprietorship means you're the sole owner. You're in charge of every decision, every move, every strategy.

Pros:

Simplicity: Setting up a sole proprietorship is relatively hassle-free. There's no need for any formal registration to start, though you might need some permits or business licenses depending on what you're up to.

Control: This is your baby. Every decision, from the color of your business card to the strategic partnerships you forge, is yours alone.

Tax Simplicity: All the business income (or losses) flows directly to your personal tax return. No need for separate business tax filings.

Cons:

Liability: The major downside? You're personally responsible for any business debts or liabilities. If things go south, your personal assets might be at risk.

Growth Potential: Sole proprietorships might face challenges when it comes to raising funds or expanding.

Final Verdict: Perfect for small-scale endeavors or if you're testing the waters of the entrepreneurial lake.

Partnerships: Sharing the Reign

What's better than one wise ruler? Two (or more)!

A partnership is a business owned by multiple individuals. Everyone contributes something, be it money, skills, labor, or a combination.

Pros:

Shared Responsibility: More hands on deck means shared responsibilities and pooled resources.

Tax Simplicity: Like sole proprietorships, business income or losses are reported on individual tax returns.

Diverse Skills: With multiple partners, you're likely to benefit from a diverse skill set.

Cons:

Liability: Unless you form a limited partnership, all partners can be held personally liable.

Disputes: More chefs in the kitchen can lead to disagreements. A clear partnership agreement is crucial.

Final Verdict: Ideal for those who believe in the adage, "Teamwork makes the dream work," but make sure you trust your partners implicitly.

Limited Liability Companies (LLC): A Hybrid Kingdom

Imagine if a sole proprietorship and a corporation had a baby. Meet the LLC!

Pros:

Flexibility: Owners, known as members, can be individuals, trusts, or even other businesses.

Liability Protection: Members aren't personally liable for the company's debts or liabilities.

Tax Options: You can choose how you'd like to be taxed, either as a sole proprietorship, partnership, or corporation.

Cons:

Complexity: While simpler than a corporation, there's still paperwork and some ongoing requirements.

Self-Employment Taxes: Members might need to pay these taxes on their share of the business profit.

Final Verdict: For those who want the liability protection of a corporation with the simplicity closer to a sole proprietorship.

Corporations: The Majestic Structures of the Business Realm

The grand castles of the business world! Corporations are separate legal entities, distinct from their owners.

Pros:

Liability Protection: Shareholders (the owners) are typically not personally liable.

Raising Capital: Easier to raise funds through the sale of stock.

Corporate Perks: Potential for fringe benefits, like health insurance.

Cons:

Complexity: More paperwork, more regulations, and more ongoing re-quirements.

Double Taxation: Corporations pay taxes on profits, and shareholders pay taxes on dividends.

Final Verdict: Suited for larger businesses with bigger ambitions, especially if looking to raise significant capital.

Comparing and Contrasting: Which Castle Suits Your Dream?

In the grand tournament of business structures, the best choice depends on your unique circumstances, ambitions, and risk tolerance.

Risk-Averse? Consider the LLC or Corporation for liability protection.

Going Solo? A Sole Proprietorship or an LLC (for added protection) might be your jam.

Got Trusted Comrades? Look into Partnerships.

Dreaming Big? Corporations are structured to help you scale.

Remember, this choice isn't static. As your business grows and evolves, you might find the need to change its structure.

Choosing the right business structure is like selecting the perfect plot of land for your castle. It requires foresight, strategic thinking, and a bit of soul-searching. But once you've laid that first stone, you're well on your way to constructing an empire that can stand the test of time. So, aspiring business royalty, let the building begin!

Crafting Your Business Identity: The Art of Branding

Ah, branding. It's the mystical force that makes us spend $5 on a cup of coffee with a siren on the cup or covet a piece of tech primarily because it's got a half-eaten fruit on the back. It's the essence, the soul, the vibe — all those intangibles that transform mere products into symbols of aspiration or belonging. Let's embark on the riveting journey of turning your business idea into a brand that sticks, resonates, and creates a legacy.

The Power of a Name: Choosing One that Resonates

"Juliet once mused, 'What's in a name?' Well, for us in the business world — a whole darn lot!"

Your brand name is more than a word. It's the first impression, the opening note in the song of your business. It can evoke emotion, imagery, and even values.

Tips for Naming Your Business:

Keep It Simple: Remember, names that are easy to say, spell, and remember have the edge.

Avoid Limitations: Don't tie yourself down. "Bob's Bagels" doesn't work if Bob wants to expand to pizzas.

Check Availability: That domain name? The social media handles? Make sure they're up for grabs.

The Takeaway: A name is more than a label; it's an ambassador for your vision.

The Right Logo: Finding a Symbol that Sticks

"Ever glanced at a tick and thought of athletic excellence or seen an apple and pondered over innovation? That's logo magic!"

Your logo is a visual shorthand, a symbol that encapsulates your brand's essence.

Creating a Memorable Logo:

Simplicity Rules: The most iconic logos aren't intricate. They're clean, adaptable, and distinctive.

Aim for Timelessness: Avoid hopping onto the latest design trend. Classics tend to last.

Versatility is Vital: Ensure it looks great everywhere, from business cards to billboards.

The Takeaway: A potent logo doesn't just identify your brand; it elevates it.

Color Psychology: How Shades Influence Perception

"Colors whisper to our subconscious. They're the silent sellers, swaying our emotions and actions."

Different colors conjure various emotions and reactions. Your brand's color palette can influence how consumers perceive and connect with you.

Harnessing the Power of Colors:

Blue: Often seen as trustworthy, dependable, and secure. Think finance or healthcare.

Red: Evokes excitement, passion, and sometimes urgency. Perfect for sales, right?

Green: Conjures thoughts of growth, freshness, and eco-friendliness.

Yellow & Orange: Optimistic, cheerful, and attention-grabbing.

The Takeaway: Your color choices paint your brand's emotional landscape. Choose with intention.

The Narrative: Telling Your Business Story

"Every brand has a tale. What's yours?

People relate to stories, not faceless corporations. Your story, whether it's how you began or what you stand for, can be a powerful tool in forming genuine connections.

Crafting Your Brand Story:

Origins Matter: Share your beginnings, struggles, and triumphs.

Stand for Something: What's your mission? What change do you wish to make?

Be Authentic: Authenticity breeds trust. Let your true self shine through.

The Takeaway: Narratives make you memorable. Make yours count.

Consistency is King: Maintaining Brand Integrity Across Platforms

"Just as a king is recognized by his crown and robe, your brand should be unmistakable everywhere."

Every touchpoint, whether it's your website, social media, or physical store, should echo the same brand elements and values.

Maintaining Consistent Branding:

Set Brand Guidelines: This includes specifics on colors, typography, and tone of voice.

Audit Regularly: Periodically check if all touchpoints align with your brand.

Train Your Team: Everyone, from the marketer to the cashier, should understand and project the brand.

The Takeaway: Consistency isn't just about recognition; it's about trust. If you look and feel the same everywhere, customers feel they "know" you.

In the grand scheme of things, branding isn't about slapping on a fancy logo or choosing snazzy colors. It's about building a legacy that stands the test of time. And now, armed with these insights, you're ready to carve out a brand identity that not only sets you apart but also leaves an indelible mark on the annals of commerce.

Charting the Terrain: Navigating Permits, Licenses, and Legalities

Embarking on a business journey comes with many exhilarating moments—seeing your idea come to life, meeting potential partners, and making those first sales. Yet, interwoven in this adventure are the less glamorous but undeniably essential components: understanding the possible permits, licenses, and legalities that might apply to your venture.

Not every business requires a permit. In fact, many entrepreneurs are pleasantly surprised to find that their specific operation doesn't need one. But here lies the importance of research: it's not about assuming you need a permit; it's about ensuring whether you do or don't. This differentiation can affect your bottom line, operational workflow, and business legitimacy. Different locales and industries have their own stipulations. For instance, while a freelance graphic designer may not need a permit, a food truck operating in the heart of the city might.

Licenses are another area to examine. A business license essentially gives you the legal authorization to begin operations. Just as with permits, specific industries have their licensing requirements. If you're delving into areas like real estate, food services, or personal care, it's crucial to get acquainted with what's expected.

The legal landscape of business can often feel like a labyrinth. It spans employment laws for hiring, contractual terms with partners or suppliers, and even intellectual property considerations if you're developing unique products or services. While it may seem daunting, each legal provision exists to provide clarity, fairness, and protection—for you, your stakeholders, and your customers.

There might be times when you find yourself in murky waters. That's where legal advisors come in. They are the lighthouses in the complex sea of business law. Whether it's clarifying a term in a contract or ensuring you're not unintentionally infringing on someone else's patent, their guidance can be invaluable. It's an investment that can preemptively address potential challenges and mitigate risks.

One final note: the business realm is ever-evolving. As industries innovate and societies progress, regulations and laws adapt in tandem. It's not just about being compliant today, but continuously ensuring that compliance. Stay updated, be part of relevant industry networks, and periodically review your status.

LAWS

Part III: Positioning, Pricing & Market Strategy

Chapter Nine

Uncovering Marketplace Gems

Terrain Survey: Setting Your Business Compass to Promising Lands

Once you've got that golden idea tucked safely in your adventurer's knapsack, it's time to scope out the perfect spot to lay its foundation. Think of it as choosing the ideal campsite after a long day's hike. You wouldn't just pitch your tent anywhere, right? Similarly, in the sprawling wilderness of the business world, finding the right terrain is crucial.

Imagine for a moment that the marketplace is an uncharted map. There are bustling market towns, quiet trade routes, and occasionally, the alluring "X" marking a treasure spot. Your task? To survey this landscape and identify where your business can thrive.

Start with your binoculars – market research. Look far and wide. What are the trends shaping the horizon? Which trade winds are other ships sailing with? Are there any looming storms you should be wary of? Data, surveys, and reports are your guiding stars here. They'll help illuminate areas where there's a demand, a gap, or even an oversupply.

Now, as any seasoned explorer would advise, while maps and tools are essential, never underestimate the power of local knowledge. Engage with potential customers, talk to fellow entrepreneurs, or even potential competitors. Their insights can be like finding a hidden trail that leads to a secret oasis.

But here's the kicker, and I can't stress this enough: just because a spot is popular doesn't mean it's right for you. Remember, you're not just looking for any terrain; you're looking for your terrain. A place where your unique business idea aligns with the needs and wants of the inhabitants.

Once you've identified a few promising spots, test the waters. Maybe set up a small stall before building a full-fledged shop. Or in tech terms, consider a soft launch or a pilot program. This trial run will give you invaluable insights and might even lead you to tweak your original idea.

To wrap it up, think of the Terrain Survey as your business's reconnaissance mission. It's about gathering intel, understanding the lay of the land, and making informed decisions.

Scouting Rival Camps: The Art of Graceful Espionage

In the vast game of commerce, it's not just about understanding your own position, but also being keenly aware of where others stand. Picture this: the marketplace is like a grand chessboard, and every move by your competitors is a strategic play that can reshape the board. To navigate this game skillfully, one must have the acumen of a chess grandmaster, always several steps ahead, always observing, always calculating.

1. The Gentleman's Spyglass: First and foremost, this isn't about corporate espionage or any underhanded tactics. It's about ethical observation. Subscribe to competitors' newsletters, follow them on social platforms, and be a silent patron to understand their offerings.

2. SWOT's Your Plan: Perform a SWOT analysis (Strengths, Weaknesses, Opportunities, Threats) on your competitors. This gives you a structured way to assess what they're excelling at and where they might be vulnerable.

3. Dive into Digital Waters: With tools like SEMrush or Ahrefs, you can peek into their online strategies. Which keywords are they targeting? What kind of content are they producing? These insights can shape your digital maneuvers.

4. Customer Chronicles: Engage in conversations with shared customers or clients. They can provide firsthand accounts of their experiences with rivals, offering you a clearer picture of the competitive landscape.

5. Attend the Grand Ball: Industry events, seminars, or conferences are splendid occasions to see competitors in action. Observe their presentations, the questions they're asked, the products or services they're showcasing.

6. The Ever-Changing Map: Remember, the competitive landscape is not static. Regularly update your knowledge, keeping tabs on any new entrants, mergers, product launches, or shifts in strategy.

Competitive observation is as much about introspection as it is about external vigilance. Every insight gleaned should lead to a reflective question: How can we do better? How can we differentiate more effectively? Where are our untapped opportunities?

In the end, scouting rival camps isn't just about understanding them; it's about refining your own strategies, sharpening your strengths, and addressing your weaknesses. It's about playing the grand game of business with finesse, strategy, and a touch of flair. As you peer across the board, always remember that while competition is a reality, excellence is a choice. Choose wisely, play smartly, and may your business always be several moves ahead.

Crafting the Jewel: The Art and Science of Perfecting Your Offerings

You've unearthed a brilliant idea and surveyed the perfect marketplace spot. Now comes one of the most exciting parts of our entrepreneurial journey: crafting your product or service. Think of this as the moment an artisan takes a raw gem and begins the meticulous process of turning it into a dazzling jewel.

So, where do we begin? Well, first things first. Every great craftsman will tell you that understanding the essence of the material you're working with is paramount. For us, this means diving deep into the core of your business idea. What problem does it solve? What value does it bring? How does it stand apart in the bustling bazaar of products and services?

Once you have a clear vision, it's time to design the first prototype. Now, I won't sugarcoat it—this phase can be a rollercoaster. There will be moments of sheer joy when things align perfectly. But there will also be times when you'll want to go back to the drawing board. Embrace it all. Every twist and turn, every high and low, is shaping your jewel to perfection.

Feedback, my dear business explorer, will be your trusted companion in this phase. Gather it like a squirrel hoarding nuts for winter. Whether it's from potential customers, mentors, or even friendly competitors, these nuggets of insight can help you refine your product or service.

Now, remember: perfection is a journey, not a destination. The business world is ever-evolving, and so are the needs and wants of consumers. This means that once you've crafted your jewel, the journey doesn't end. It's an ongoing process of refining, adapting, and polishing to ensure that your offering remains as dazzling as ever.

In conclusion, crafting your product or service is a dance between artistry and pragmatism. It demands creativity, resilience, and a keen ear to the market's heartbeat. But as you hold your crafted jewel up to the light, watching it shimmer and shine, you'll realize: every effort, every revision, every late night was worth it. Here's to the artisans of the business world, crafting legacies one jewel at a time!

Quality Inspection: The Business Jeweler's Final Touch

Picture this: a master jeweler, magnifying glass in hand, meticulously inspecting a gleaming piece for any imperfections. Each facet, every angle, scrutinized with precision. This, dear entrepreneur, mirrors the vital step in our business journey - the Quality Inspection.

Now, having passionately crafted your product or service, it's tempting to rush it into the marketplace. But hold your horses! Just like a jeweler would never showcase a piece without a thorough inspection, you must ensure that your offering is nothing short of impeccable.

So, how do we go about this?

1. The Self-Review: Start with an honest evaluation. Look at your product or service from every angle. Test it, use it, experience it. Would you buy it? If the answer is a resounding 'yes', you're on the right track.

2. Peer Perspectives: Sometimes, a fresh pair of eyes can spot what we might overlook. Rope in some trusted peers or mentors. Their insights, drawn from their own entrepreneurial escapades, can be invaluable.

3. Customer Trials: Consider offering your product or service for free, do a soft launch or a beta test. Real feedback from real customers or users is worth its weight in gold. Listen closely to their experiences, their praises, and especially their critiques.

4. The Checklist Challenge: Create a comprehensive checklist. Everything from functionality, aesthetics, to user experience should be on it. Tick them off one by one, ensuring that each aspect of your offering meets the high standards you've set.

5. Adapt and Evolve: Remember, quality isn't a one-time checkmark; it's an ongoing commitment. As you gather more feedback and as the market dynamics shift, be ready to make tweaks to ensure your product or service remains top-notch.

Pricing Calibration: The Delicate Dance of Value and Worth

Stepping into the bustling marketplace of business, one of the most intricate puzzles every entrepreneur faces is the challenge of pricing. It's not just a number—it's a statement. It tells your customers what you believe your product or service is worth and, more importantly, what value it holds for them.

Pricing isn't just about slapping on a tag. It's an artful balance between understanding your worth, gauging market dynamics, and recognizing the value you offer to your customers. It's about answering that age-old question: "What's the right price?"

Let's embark on this exciting calibration journey together:

1. Cost Analysis: Before we set sail, let's anchor ourselves in basics. Understand the costs involved in creating your product or service. From raw materials, labor, to overheads, get a clear picture of what goes into your offering.

2. Market Research: Dive deep into the waters of your industry. What are your competitors charging? Where does your product stand in the grand spectrum? Remember, while it's essential to stay competitive, a race to the bottom isn't always the answer.

3. Value Proposition: This is where the magic happens. What unique value does your product or service offer? Are you saving your customers time? Offering unparalleled quality? Or perhaps, an experience like no other? Your price should reflect this intrinsic value.

4. Elasticity Exploration: Some products have what we call 'price elasticity'. Essentially, how do changes in price impact demand? For some, a minor price increase might lead to significant sales drops, while others remain unaffected. Knowing where your product stands can be a game-changer.

5. Psychological Pricing: Ever wondered why products are often priced at $9.99 instead of $10? There's a science behind it! Delving into the psychology of pricing can offer insights into how customers perceive different price points.

6. Feedback & Flexibility: Once you've set a price, gather feedback. Are customers finding it reasonable? Too high? Too low? And be ready to pivot. The best entrepreneurs are those who listen and adapt.

In wrapping up, pricing calibration is much like a dance. It's about rhythm, balance, and understanding your partner - in this case, the market and your customer. It's about not underselling yourself but also ensuring that your customers see and appreciate the value they're getting.

Claiming Your Spot: Planting Your Flag in the Business Frontier

Imagine the early pioneers, navigating vast landscapes, facing unknown challenges, and eventually finding that perfect spot to call home. They'd plant their flag, stake their claim, and begin building. In the world of business, this is akin to establishing a unique market presence amidst a sea of competitors. It's about making your mark, letting the world know you've arrived, and you're here to stay.

But how does one go about this? How do you ensure that amidst the cacophony of business voices, yours stands out, distinct and memorable? Let's set out on this adventure to claim your rightful spot:

1. Know Thyself: Before you shout from the rooftops, understand your core message. What does your brand stand for? What promise are you making to your customers? Having clarity here is the cornerstone of a strong market presence.

2. Uniqueness is Gold: In a world of replicas, being original is priceless. Identify what sets you apart. It could be your product, your service, your ethos, or even the story behind your brand.

3. Consistency is Key: Whether it's the tone of your communications, the look of your branding, or the quality of your offerings, maintaining consistency ensures you're instantly recognizable in the market.

4. Engage & Listen: Engage with your audience. Understand their needs, their feedback, their aspirations.

5. Collaborate to Elevate: Consider partnerships or collaborations that align with your brand. This can not only boost your presence but introduce you to new audiences.

Chapter Ten

Carving Out a Market Niche

Adapting the Caravan's Route: Navigating the Shifting Sands of Business

In the expanse of the business world, entrepreneurs often find themselves on a journey, much like a caravan weaving its way through uncharted terrains. And while the skies above are dotted with stars, offering guidance and direction, the path below is constantly shifting, presenting both challenges and opportunities.

The route, at the outset, might seem clear. The destination is set, and the path ahead is filled with the promise of discovery. But, much like the desert terrains, the business landscape is in constant flux. Market trends and consumer preferences can be as unpredictable as desert winds, changing the course and demanding adaptability.

But how does a caravan, or in this case, a business, navigate these ever-changing conditions? The answer lies in adaptability and the willingness to chart new courses.

To ensure the journey's success, it's essential to have scouts. In the world of business, these scouts manifest as research and development teams, the forward-thinkers who keep an eye on the horizon, anticipating changes and challenges. They are the ones who notice the subtle shifts in the sands, be it a new competitor on the horizon, a technological advancement that reshapes an industry, or global events that can create unexpected market storms.

As these scouts relay their findings, communication becomes paramount. Every member of the caravan, from the leaders to the traders, must be aligned with any changes in direction or strategy. In a business context, this means ensuring that all departments, from marketing to production, are on the same page, ready to pivot or accelerate as the situation demands.

Sometimes, this adaptability may involve taking a detour, choosing a path that might be longer but is more aligned with the company's values and goals. At other times, it could mean seizing an emerging opportunity, even if it means racing ahead.

Throughout these strategic shifts, the ultimate goal remains unaltered: reaching the intended destination. In the realm of business, this translates to staying true to the company's mission and vision, even when navigating the most challenging terrains.

The success of the journey isn't defined solely by the destination but by the adaptability and resilience shown along the way. By understanding that the path may change, but the drive and spirit remain unwavering, businesses, like caravans, can find their way through the most daunting landscapes, guided by the stars above and the wisdom they've gathered below.

Showcasing the Best Wares: Unveiling the Value of Your Offerings

Think of your business offerings as the handcrafted artifacts of olden times, each piece meticulously designed and crafted. They aren't just products or services; they are the culmination of passion, dedication, and expertise. To truly showcase their unique value, it's not enough to simply display them; one must narrate their tale, their origin, their purpose.

Start by understanding your creation. Dive deep into what makes it stand out. Is it the unmatched quality? Perhaps it's the innovative design or the problem it solves for the consumer. Once you've pinpointed its distinctive features, it's time to weave the narrative, the story that sets it apart.

But remember, in the marketplace it's not just about the product; it's about the experience. It's the way you engage with potential buyers, the passion in your voice, the authenticity of your pitch. Your offerings might be top-notch, but it's the way you present them, with confidence and charisma, that will truly make them irresistible.

Consider the art of demonstration. Let the audience feel, touch, or experience the product. A hands-on encounter can often be more persuasive than the most eloquent of speeches. Show them the tangible benefits, the real-world applications, and let the product speak for itself.

Feedback is gold. Pay attention to what the market is saying. Are there specific features they love? Or perhaps there's an aspect they feel could be improved? By listening and adapting, you ensure that your wares remain relevant and in demand.

Consistent Quality: The Unwavering Luster of Business Excellence

Quality isn't just a one-time achievement; it's a commitment, an ongoing promise. It's the assurance that every time a customer engages with your product or service, they'll receive the same exceptional experience. This consistency builds trust, turning casual customers into loyal advocates.

Imagine for a moment a craftsman meticulously shaping and polishing a gem. Each facet is carefully considered, each angle honed to perfection. Now, think of that craftsman producing not just one, but thousands of such gems, each as brilliant as the last. This is the challenge businesses face daily. In a world of mass production and automation, maintaining that handcrafted touch, that unwavering standard, is no small feat.

But why is consistent quality so pivotal? Because it's the bedrock of a brand's reputation. In an age where word of mouth can spread at the speed of light, thanks to social media, a single misstep can tarnish years of goodwill. Conversely, a steadfast commitment to quality can elevate a brand, setting it on a pedestal in the minds of consumers.

Achieving this consistency requires more than just stringent quality checks. It demands a culture of excellence, where every team member, from the boardroom to the factory floor, is aligned with the brand's ethos. It's about instilling pride in one's work, fostering a mindset where good enough simply isn't enough.

In the end, consistent quality is a journey, not a destination. It's a relentless pursuit, a drive to constantly raise the bar. And while the path might be strewn with challenges, the rewards — customer loyalty, brand prestige, and market leadership — are well worth the effort. For in business, it's the threads of consistent quality that truly make a brand shine brilliantly, standing out as a gem in a sea of stones.

Beyond Competition: The Uncelebrated Spirit of Cooperation in Business

In the world of business, the spotlight often shines brightest on competition. The narrative of fierce rivals, battling it out in a gladiatorial arena, captures imaginations. Capitalism, in popular discourse, is painted as a relentless 'dog-eat-dog' world where only the fittest survive. But behind the curtains, away from the limelight, lies a story less told but equally powerful: the story of cooperation.

At its core, business isn't just about outdoing one another; it's about working together towards shared goals. The skyscrapers that punctuate our cityscapes? They weren't built by a single entity but were the result of countless professionals — architects, engineers, laborers, and more — collaborating harmoniously.

Consider the intricate web of global trade. Goods produced in one corner of the world find their way to consumers thousands of miles away. This isn't the result of cutthroat competition but intricate partnerships between manufacturers, shippers, retailers, and many others.

Innovation, too, thrives not just in isolation but in collaboration. The tech hubs of the world, from Silicon Valley to Bangalore, are buzzing hives of shared ideas. Startups collaborate with giants, competitors become partners, and out of this melting pot of cooperation emerge products and services that shape the future.

This cooperative spirit isn't a modern phenomenon. Historically, merchants on ancient trade routes would form caravans, not just for safety but to share knowledge about diverse markets. Artisans in medieval guilds collaborated to hone their crafts and set quality standards.

So, why then does the narrative of fierce competition overshadow cooperation? Perhaps because rivalry is dramatic, easily sensationalized. But those in the trenches of business know the truth. They understand that while competition drives excellence, cooperation breeds sustainability and growth.

It's also worth noting that today's consumers are more discerning. They gravitate towards businesses that prioritize community over competition, that value collaboration over cutthroat practices. Brands that uplift others, that champion cooperative values, resonate more deeply in a world yearning for connection.

In essence, the heart of business beats to a rhythm of both competition and cooperation. While the competitive spirit pushes boundaries and challenges the status quo, cooperation builds bridges and fosters a sense of community. As we move forward, it's crucial to celebrate not just the battles won in the marketplace but also the alliances formed, the partnerships forged, and the collective victories achieved through cooperation. For in the dance of business, competition might lead, but cooperation sets the tempo.

Building Trade Bonds: Nurturing Trust and Forging Partnerships in the Marketplace

Forming bonds and partnerships isn't just a strategic move; it's a survival tactic. First and foremost, trust is the cornerstone of any partnership. It's not built overnight but is nurtured over time through consistent actions, transparency, and mutual respect. As a trader, your word is your bond. Honoring commitments, delivering quality, and maintaining integrity are non-negotiables.

But trust isn't just about keeping promises; it's also about vulnerability. It's about admitting when you don't have all the answers and leaning on others for their expertise. It's about sharing successes and shouldering failures together. In the intricate dance of business partnerships, trust leads the way.

Once trust is established, the next step is collaboration. Look for synergies. Perhaps your offerings complement another trader's products, creating a package deal that's irresistible to customers. Or maybe pooling resources can lead to shared marketing campaigns or bulk purchasing benefits. The possibilities are as vast as the marketplace itself.

However, not all partnerships are about direct collaboration. Sometimes, it's about mentorship. Seasoned traders, with their wealth of experience, can offer guidance and insights to newcomers. In return, fresh perspectives and innovative ideas from newer traders can breathe new life into established businesses.

Networking is key. Attend industry events, join trader guilds, or participate in community workshops. These are goldmines for potential partnerships. But remember, it's not just about quantity but quality. Seek out traders whose values align with yours, whose vision resonates with your own.

Lastly, celebrate successes together. When one trader thrives, it lifts the entire marketplace. Share stories, exchange notes, and toast to milestones. In this ever-evolving world of business, relationships are the anchors that provide stability and support.

Behind the Curtains: Building a Robust, Responsive Supply Chain

Building a robust and responsive supply chain is a foundational pillar for any successful business that handles physical goods. This involves navigating the landscape of potential suppliers to find those who not only uphold the highest standards of quality but also align with your business's vision and ethos. While established names bring credibility and reliability, emerging suppliers can offer flexibility, innovation, and a fresh perspective.

Once partners are in place, the next step is to streamline operations. Understanding market demands is crucial. This can be achieved by delving deep into research, analyzing past sales trajectories, and staying attuned to current market trends. Mastery over inventory management is essential. Ensuring that you have the right amount of stock—neither too much nor too little—can be the difference between profit and loss.

However, even the best-planned operations can face unexpected challenges. In the world of business, unpredictability is a constant. Therefore, regular reviews and stress-testing of your supply chain processes are vital. By doing so, you can prepare for known challenges and also devise strategies for unforeseen setbacks. For instance, if a key supplier faces a disruption or if there's a sudden surge in demand, having a plan in place ensures continuity and resilience.

Lastly, the business landscape is ever-evolving. To remain relevant and competitive, continuous adaptation and innovation are necessary. This involves nurturing relationships with suppliers, viewing them as valued collaborators rather than just vendors. Moreover, listening to customer feedback and incorporating their insights can lead to improvements, innovations, and sustained growth.

Part IV: Building Your Dream Team & Enhancing the Customer Experience

Chapter Eleven

Recruiting and Growing a Winning Team

Starting Small but Strong: The Freelancer and Virtual Assistant Route

Embarking on the entrepreneurial journey often begins as a solo expedition. The thrill of building something from the ground up, the initial stages of setting the foundation, and the excitement of seeing your vision take shape are unparalleled. However, as the path unfolds, there may come a point where the tasks begin to pile up, and the hours in the day seem insufficient. Yet, you might feel you're not quite ready to assemble a full-fledged team. If you find yourself at this crossroads, there's a middle path that offers the best of both worlds: hiring freelancers and virtual assistants (VAs).

Think of freelancers and VAs as seasoned travelers you can hire for specific legs of your journey. They come with their own set of tools, expertise, and flexibility, allowing you to navigate certain terrains more efficiently. They're perfect for those times when you need an extra set of hands but aren't looking for a permanent crew member.

The beauty of this approach lies in its adaptability. Need a logo for your fledgling online store? A freelance graphic designer can create a custom design that captures your brand's essence. Overwhelmed by customer inquiries about your new product line on social media? A virtual assistant (VA) can manage your inbox, ensuring every potential customer receives a timely response.

At marketplaces like Upwork and Fiverr you can find freelancers equipped for almost any task you can envision. These platforms, combined with clear communication and a shared understanding of your venture's ethos, can lead to fruitful collaborations.

And who knows? Over time, these temporary collaborators might showcase a dedication and alignment with your vision so profound that they transition into full-time employees, becoming integral parts of your growing team.

However, it's important to navigate this path with discernment. While freelancers and VAs can cover vast grounds, there are certain terrains best traversed personally, especially when they lie at the heart of your venture. Strategic decisions, core business planning, and areas requiring intimate knowledge of your brand's essence are journeys you'll want to undertake yourself.

Discovering Diamonds: Where to Find Your Team

Taking the leap to hire your first employee? It's a thrilling milestone! While familiar avenues like job boards and recruitment agencies have their merits, venturing beyond the conventional can often lead you to uncover truly standout candidates..

Traditional Avenues:

LinkedIn and Job Boards: Platforms like LinkedIn, Indeed, and Glassdoor have become staples in the recruitment process. They offer a vast pool of candidates, each with detailed profiles, recommendations, and work samples. By posting a job ad or even searching for potential fits, you can tap into a wide range of talent. Don't underestimate the power of a well-crafted job post, one that genuinely speaks to your company's values and vision.

Recruitment Agencies: These agencies have extensive networks and can quickly connect you with potential candidates. They do the initial screening, ensuring you only see candidates that fit your criteria.

University and College Career Fairs: These are perfect if you're looking for fresh talent, eager to start their professional journey. Engaging with educational institutions can also set the stage for internships or apprenticeships.

The Road Less Traveled: Creative Strategies

Networking Events and Seminars: Beyond the formal job-seeking platforms, events related to your industry can be goldmines. Not only do you get to meet potential candidates in a more relaxed setting, but you also get a feel for how they fit within the industry community.

Talent Showcases or Hackathons: Depending on your industry, participating in or hosting events where skills are put to the test can be an excellent way to spot talent. For tech companies, hackathons can reveal brilliant coders. For design firms, portfolio showcases can highlight emerging artists.

Employee Referrals: Sometimes, your current team can be the best scout. They understand the company culture and might know someone from their network who'd be a perfect fit.

Social Media Scouting: Platforms like Instagram or Twitter aren't just for leisure. Artists showcase portfolios on Instagram, while thought leaders share insights on Twitter. Engage with their content, and you might just find your next star employee.

Workshops and Classes: Offering or attending workshops can be a dual-purpose strategy. While you impart or gain knowledge, you also get to interact with attendees, some of whom might be looking for opportunities or know someone who is.

Remember, while the destination is to find the perfect candidate, the journey matters too. Each interaction, whether it leads to a hire or not, enhances your brand's reputation and network. Approach each avenue with an open mind and genuine interest, and soon enough, you'll find the talent that resonates with your brand's heartbeat.

The Art of Selecting a Team that Resonates with Your Brand's Ethos

Every business owner knows that their company is only as strong as the team behind it. Think of building your team like casting for a blockbuster movie. You wouldn't just want talented actors; you'd want actors who fit the roles, who embody the essence of the characters they portray. Similarly, when selecting team members for your business, it's imperative to find individuals who not only possess the necessary skills but also resonate with your brand's core values and mission.

First and foremost, it's vital to have a clear understanding of your brand's ethos. What does your brand stand for? What are its core values? Once you have a solid grasp of this, you can begin the process of selecting team members who align with these principles.

Start with the job description. While it's crucial to outline the technical requirements and skills needed for the position, also emphasize the importance of cultural fit. Mention your brand's values and mission. Make it clear that you're not just looking for someone who can do the job but someone who believes in what the company stands for.

During the interview process, ask open-ended questions that allow candidates to express their personal values and beliefs. Questions like, "What drives you?" or "Tell me about a time when you had to stand up for something you believed in at work," can provide valuable insights into a candidate's character and whether they'd be a good fit for your brand.

It's also beneficial to include scenarios or role-playing exercises in the interview. Present a situation that tests both their skills and their alignment with your brand values. How they handle these scenarios can be very telling.

Remember, skills can be taught, but a person's core beliefs and values are deeply ingrained. By placing emphasis on cultural fit and brand alignment from the outset, you're more likely to assemble a team that not only works well together but also passionately upholds and advances your brand's mission.

In the end, the goal is to build a cohesive unit, a team where every member is on the same page, moving in the same direction, and working towards the same objectives. When you achieve this level of synergy, your business won't just succeed; it will thrive.

The Role of the Maestro: Leadership in Ensuring Harmony and Synchronization

In the orchestra of a thriving business, every instrument plays a vital role. From the soft melodies of the flutes to the commanding beats of the drums, each note contributes to the symphony's overall beauty. But above all this, guiding every movement and ensuring each section comes in at the right moment, stands the Maestro. In the world of business, this Maestro is the leader.

Imagine, for a moment, an orchestra without its conductor. The violins might rush ahead, the trumpets could come in too loudly, and the entire performance could easily descend into chaos. Similarly, a business without strong, decisive leadership can quickly lose its rhythm and direction.

The Maestro doesn't just wave a baton aimlessly; every movement is calculated, every gesture designed to bring out the best in the orchestra. Similarly, effective leaders don't merely issue commands; they inspire, motivate, and guide their teams towards a shared vision.

A leader understands the strengths and weaknesses of each team member, much like how a Maestro knows which violinist can deliver a solo flawlessly or which section needs a little more practice. They provide the necessary resources, be it training for an employee or more rehearsal time for a section of the orchestra, ensuring that when the curtain rises, the performance is nothing short of spectacular.

But being a Maestro isn't just about knowing the score inside out. It's about feeling the music, understanding its soul. In business, this translates to a leader being genuinely passionate about the company's mission. It's this passion that ignites the same fire in their team, driving them to give their best performance every single day.

Yet, even as they command the stage, the Maestro remains humble, always learning, always growing. They listen, not just to the music but to the silence between the notes, always seeking feedback and looking for areas of improvement. In the business realm, the most successful leaders are those who seek feedback, who aren't afraid to admit their mistakes, and who view every setback as a learning opportunity.

As the symphony reaches its crescendo, the Maestro and the orchestra are in perfect sync, their energies feeding off each other. In businesses that thrive, you'll find a similar relationship between the leader and the team. A mutual respect, a shared goal, and an unbreakable bond that drives them towards success.

In the end, while the instruments create the music, it's the Maestro's guidance that shapes it, molds it, and turns it into a masterpiece. Just as in a flourishing business, it's the leader's vision and dedication that transform individual efforts into a harmonious, synchronized success story. So, if you aspire to lead, strive to be the Maestro, guiding your team to create beautiful symphonies day after day.

SUCCESS

Chapter Twelve

It's All About the Customer Experience

Personalizing Interactions for an Unforgettable Experience

Every individual who interacts with your business brings with them a unique set of preferences, experiences, and expectations. Recognizing and valuing this uniqueness becomes particularly crucial when the products or services you offer come with a higher price tag. When a customer is investing a significant sum, say $1000, they expect an interaction that matches the value of their investment. They seek to be seen and understood, not as a mere number but as a person, and their engagement with your brand deepens when this need is met.

However, for more economically priced items, say something that costs $5, extensive personalization might not only be unrealistic but also impractical. The cost and effort of tailoring interactions for such products could outweigh the benefits. Instead, for these items, efficiency, consistency, and reliability become the focal points.

Listening, truly listening, to your customers is foundational. By immersing yourself in their feedback, understanding their needs, and anticipating their desires, you can tailor your offerings and services to resonate more profoundly with them, especially for premium products. It's akin to having a conversation where, instead of speaking over one another, you're in sync, responding to cues, and building upon each shared insight.

The business landscape is ever-evolving, and with it, the needs and preferences of customers shift. Staying adaptable, being willing to pivot, and embracing change are crucial. This dynamic approach ensures that you remain relevant, meeting your customers where they are and delivering value consistently.

But amidst all this, it's essential to carve out a unique space for your business, something distinctive that sets you apart. It could be the unparalleled quality of your products, the responsiveness of your customer service, or the ethos that underpins your brand. This uniqueness becomes the beacon, drawing customers to you and fostering loyalty.

I understand I might sound like a broken record at this point, but it's a tune that's perhaps the most crucial in your business endeavor: Feedback is the North Star guiding your entrepreneurial voyage. Proactively embracing customer insights paints a vivid picture of what's resonating and what needs a second look. This continuous dance of feedback and refinement ensures that your business stays in sync with its audience's rhythm.

Taking a Bow and Listening: Gathering Feedback Post-Performance (After Sales)

Once the proverbial curtains fall and the spotlight dims, the performance might be over, but the journey isn't. The act of "taking a bow" in business isn't just about acknowledging a job well done; it's an opportune moment to lean in and listen. As with any performance, it's the audience's reaction that truly measures success, and in the realm of business, this translates to post-sales feedback from customers. While we've touched upon the importance of feedback before, let's delve into the mechanics of gathering and evaluating it effectively.

1. Surveys and Questionnaires:

Crafting concise and targeted surveys can offer invaluable insights. Utilizing platforms like SurveyMonkey or Google Forms allows for easy distribution and data collection. Remember to keep questions clear and to the point, ensuring respondents don't experience survey fatigue.

2. Feedback Forums:

Creating a dedicated space on your website or platform for customers to share their experiences can be beneficial. Not only does it provide direct insights, but it also fosters a community where customers can interact and share opinions.

3. Social Media Listening:

Platforms like Mention or Brandwatch can help monitor mentions of your brand across social media. These tools can capture real-time sentiments, giving you a pulse on customer opinions as they unfold.

4. Focus Groups:

For a deeper dive into customer opinions, consider organizing focus groups. This method allows for a more nuanced understanding, capturing not just the what, but also the why behind customer feedback.

5. Review Platforms:

Sites like Trustpilot, Yelp, or Google Reviews are where many customers voice their experiences. Regularly monitoring and responding to these can provide insights and also showcase your brand's commitment to customer satisfaction.

6. Analytical Tools:

Using tools like Net Promoter Score (NPS) can quantify customer satisfaction. It's a straightforward metric that measures the likelihood of customers to recommend your product or service to others.

7. Direct Communication:

Never underestimate the power of a personal touch. Reaching out directly, be it through phone calls, emails, or even face-to-face interactions, can yield rich insights. It shows customers you genuinely value their opinion, strengthening brand loyalty.

The Revision Room: Analyzing Feedback for Actionable Insights

Begin with the art of distillation. Amidst the vast sea of feedback, it's essential to discern the recurring patterns and standout points. This is where raw feedback morphs into structured data, giving you a clearer picture of sentiments. Visualization tools can play a pivotal role, transforming words and numbers into graphs and charts that paint a coherent narrative.

However, remember that not all feedback is created equal. While every piece holds value, some are more pressing or impactful than others. Prioritizing feedback involves carefully weighing its frequency, potential business impact, and the feasibility of implementation.

Feedback also exists within a broader context. It's not just about what's said but also about understanding the 'why' behind it. This means looking at feedback against the canvas of current market trends, the competitive landscape, and internal business metrics. Perhaps you receive suggestions on enhancing a product feature, but if the larger market is pivoting away from that attribute, it warrants deeper introspection.

The process of analyzing feedback should be a collective endeavor. Engaging teams across various departments, from product design to marketing, can offer a richer, more nuanced understanding. Everyone brings a unique lens, and this diversity can unearth insights that might otherwise remain hidden.

Once these insights are gleaned, the journey isn't over. It's merely the start of a continuous feedback loop. It's about implementing changes, gauging their effectiveness, refining, and then iterating. This cyclical process ensures that the business remains agile and responsive.

Documenting these insights is of paramount importance. By creating a record, you're building a repository of knowledge, a treasure trove that future decisions can draw upon. Sharing these findings ensures that all teams, regardless of their function, move in harmony, aligned in their understanding and purpose.

Occasionally, it might also prove beneficial to seek an external perspective. Industry experts or consultants can offer an objective viewpoint, free from the inherent biases that come with being closely tied to a project or product. Their fresh insights can illuminate areas previously overlooked.

Part V: Amplifying Your Impact: Marketing & Expansion

Chapter Thirteen

Finding Your Voice: The Marketing Blueprint

The Importance of Marketing for Small Businesses

Imagine you've whipped up the most delectable chocolate cake the world has ever seen. It's rich, it's moist, and it's got layers upon layers of chocolatey goodness. But here's the kicker – if nobody knows about your cake, it's just going to sit there, no matter how delicious it is. And that's a crying shame.

This is where marketing comes into play. It's the loudspeaker that announces to the world, "Hey, come and get a slice of this!" For a small business, marketing isn't just about selling products or services; it's about telling a story, sharing your passion, and connecting with people who believe in what you do. It's about making sure that delectable cake you baked doesn't just sit there; it gets the appreciation (and sales) it deserves!

The Four 4Ps in Marketing

Alright, let's talk about a classic concept that's as timeless as grandma's secret recipes – the 4Ps of Marketing. These are the fundamental pillars that form the foundation of any robust marketing strategy:

Product: This is the heart of your business. Whether it's a tangible item like handcrafted jewelry or a service like event planning, it's crucial to understand its features, benefits, and the problems it solves for your customers.

Price: Ah, the art of pricing! It's a balancing act. Set it too high, and you might scare customers away; too low, and you might not make a profit. It's about understanding the market, your competition, and the value you offer.

Place: This is all about distribution. Where are you selling your product? A quaint brick-and-mortar shop downtown? An online store? Maybe both? It's essential to be where your customers are.

Promotion: How are you going to get the word out? Will you run a cheeky ad campaign, or perhaps rely on word-of-mouth and stellar reviews? Maybe a bit of influencer marketing? It's all about creating a buzz.

Once upon a time, businesses relied on grand billboards, catchy radio jingles, and vibrant newspaper ads. That was the age of traditional marketing.

Now, we're talking about eye-catching Instagram posts, viral tweets, engaging blogs, and oh-so-satisfying product videos. Digital marketing allows you to reach a global audience, interact with customers in real-time, and gather insights using analytics.

However, it's not about picking one over the other. For many businesses, a mix of traditional and digital marketing works wonders. It's like mixing old-school charm with new-age flair.

Starting a small business is a thrilling roller coaster ride. There will be ups, and there will be downs. But with the right marketing strategies in your toolkit, you're setting yourself up for success. Remember, marketing isn't just about selling; it's about connecting, sharing, and building relationships. It's a beautiful dance between art and science, creativity and analytics.

Identifying Your Target Audience

Think of the market as a big, delicious pie. Now, as much as we'd love to, we can't eat the whole pie at once. We need to slice it. Market segmentation is just that — slicing your market into manageable, bite-sized pieces that you can effectively target.

Demographic Segmentation: This is all about the numbers and facts. We're talking age, gender, income, education, and so on. For instance, if you're selling luxury handbags, you might target women in a higher income bracket.

Geographic Segmentation: Location, location, location! Whether it's city dwellers or country folks, beach bums or mountain enthusiasts, where your customers are can influence their buying decisions.

Psychographic Segmentation: Dive deep into the minds of your audience. What are their values, hobbies, lifestyle choices, and personalities? Maybe your eco-friendly products resonate with those leading a sustainable lifestyle.

Behavioral Segmentation: How do your customers behave? Are they loyal brand enthusiasts or bargain hunters? Do they make impulse purchases or research extensively before buying?

Imagine if your target audience came to life as vivid characters. Meet Tina, a 28-year-old urbanite who loves staying updated with the latest fashion. Or Eco Eddie, a 35-year-old nature lover who's all about sustainable living. These are customer personas — fictional, yet based on real data, representations of your ideal customers. Crafting these personas helps you visualize your audience, making it easier to tailor your marketing strategies. It's like having a friendly chat with Tina or Eddie, understanding their needs, and offering solutions.

In the world of business, understanding your ideal customer is incredibly important. It helps tailor your products, fine-tune your marketing strategies, and even decide where to sell. It's about forging genuine connections, making your customers feel seen and understood. When you hit that sweet spot, you're not just selling a product; you're offering value, building trust, and creating loyal brand advocates.

The Unique Selling Point Potion: Brewing Your Own Magic

USP, or Unique Selling Point, is the special touch your business brings to the table. It's the signature flair that makes you, well, uniquely you. It's the answer to that ever-present question echoing in customers' minds: "What makes you the choice I should pick amidst the crowd?"

Creating your USP is like brewing a potent potion. It requires a mix of understanding your product's strengths, knowing your audience's desires, and sprinkling in a dash of market awareness.

Now, having a USP is fantastic, but it's just one piece of the jigsaw. The bigger picture? Positioning your business in the market. Imagine your business as a vibrant painting, and positioning is choosing exactly where to hang it in a gallery full of artworks. It determines how your audience perceives you in relation to competitors.

How do you want to be seen? As the affordable, go-to choice for the masses? Or perhaps the premium, luxury option for the few? Positioning is about carving a distinct space in the market landscape and ensuring your brand's voice echoes loud and clear.

Sculpting Your USP and Positioning: A Step-by-Step Guide

Deep Dive into Your Offering: Understand your product or service inside out. What features make it special? Is it the relatability, the personal touch, the handcrafted quality, the innovative tech, or maybe the stellar after-sales service?

Know Thy Audience: What does your ideal customer value most? Speed, quality, cost, or perhaps sustainability?

Scope Out the Neighbors: Observe your competitors. What are they boasting about? Find gaps in their offerings and see if you can fill them.

Marry Your Strengths with Their Desires: This is where the magic happens. Combine what you do best with what your audience craves. Voila! You've got your USP.

Consistency is Key: Once you've sculpted your USP and positioning, be consistent. Whether it's your marketing campaigns, product packaging, or customer interactions, let your USP shine through.

Referral Programs: Amplifying the Whisper of Word-of-Mouth

There's an old saying that if you do something good, one person might tell another. But mess up, and they'll tell ten others. In today's hyper-connected world, those numbers have skyrocketed. Fortunately, when it comes to spreading the good word about your business, referral programs can turn that whisper of positive chatter into a booming announcement.

Picture this: You're at a dinner party, and your friend can't stop raving about this new cafe downtown. The ambiance, the coffee, the pastries—everything gets a glowing review. Now, you've never seen an ad for this cafe, nor have you read about it. But based on your friend's passionate recommendation, guess where you're heading for breakfast the next day?

That's the magic of word-of-mouth—a genuine, heartfelt recommendation from someone you trust. But what if, as a business owner, you could harness this organic enthusiasm and give it a little nudge? That's where referral programs come in.

A referral program is like handing your loyal customers a megaphone and asking them to shout out about your brand from the rooftops. But instead of asking them to do it out of the goodness of their hearts, you incentivize them. Maybe it's a discount on their next purchase, a freebie, or some exclusive perks. Whatever the reward, the essence remains the same: "If you love our product or service, tell your friends and family. And when they come through your recommendation, both of you get rewarded!"

Now, before you jump on the referral bandwagon, here are some golden nuggets to keep in mind:

Keep It Simple: Your customers aren't treasure hunters. Make sure your referral process is straightforward. A complex process with too many steps can deter even your most loyal patrons.

Make It Worthwhile: If you're asking customers to vouch for your brand, make sure the reward is enticing. It doesn't always have to be monetary. Early access to a new product or an exclusive webinar can also do the trick.

Double the Joy: The best referral programs reward both the referrer and the referred. It's like hosting a party where both the person bringing a guest and the guest leave with a goodie bag.

Celebrate & Showcase: Got a customer who's referred ten friends? Celebrate them! Maybe even feature them on your social media. It not only makes them feel valued but also encourages others to get on the referral train.

Track & Tweak: Use analytics to track the success of your referral program. Which rewards are most popular? At what point do users drop out of the referral process? These insights can help you refine and optimize for even better results.

Chapter Fourteen

Mastering the Digital Frontier

Content Creation & Social Media Safari

Dive deep into the world of business, and you'll soon realize there's a currency more valuable than money: trust. In this age where everyone is vying for attention, the question isn't just about how loud you can shout, but what you're saying. Enter the world of content marketing, where your brand's voice isn't just heard—it resonates.

Let's imagine your business as a bustling city. Your products and services? They're the skyscrapers and landmarks. But what about the roads that lead people to them? That's your content. Think of content marketing as laying down these pathways, guiding potential clients to your offerings while giving them scenic views along the way.

But how does one craft content that doesn't just get scrolled past? Here's the secret sauce: authenticity mixed with value. Your content should evoke a feeling, answer a question, or solve a problem. When readers find genuine value in what you share, they don't just consume it—they share it, spreading your brand's message organically.

Valuable content establishes another important thing: authority. Imagine walking into a room where you're seen as the go-to expert on a subject. That's the aura your content should create for your brand. When customers trust you to provide insights, they'll trust you with their business needs.

Let's embark on a whirlwind tour of the social media landscape, shall we? First stop: Facebook, the behemoth platform where diverse demographics mingle. It's a haven for community-building, from groups to pages dedicated to niche interests. Next, we take a look at Instagram and TikTok, the visual wonderlands, where aesthetics reign supreme. This is where you woo your audience with dazzling videos, images and intimate stories. Twitter, with its rapid-fire dialogue, is where you establish thought leadership and engage in real-time conversations. LinkedIn, the professional hub, is perfect for B2B interactions, while Pinterest, with its mood boards, is a haven for brands aiming to inspire.

Creating content for these platforms is both an art and a science. It's not about being everywhere but being impactful wherever you are. Craft posts that resonate, engage, and, most importantly, align with your brand's voice. Dive into the immersive world of stories on Instagram and Facebook, giving followers a behind-the-scenes peek. Embrace the candid charm of reels or TikToks, and if you're feeling particularly adventurous, go live! Engage with your audience in real-time, answer questions, and build a genuine rapport.

In the ever-evolving world of social media marketing, remember this golden rule: It's not about speaking to the masses, but having meaningful conversations with the individual. So, craft, curate, and connect. After all, in this digital dance, it's all about moving to the rhythm of your audience's heartbeats.

Imagine you've crafted the most delightful, engaging piece of content. Now, how do you ensure that it doesn't just linger in the vast expanses of the internet, waiting to be discovered?

Boosted posts, targeted campaigns, carousel ads—the options are myriad. The key is to target not just anyone, but the right someone. Understand your audience's demographics, behaviors, and preferences, and tailor your campaigns accordingly.

Another option are pay-per-click (PPC) campaigns. It's a model where you essentially bid for your advertisement's placement in search engine's sponsored links. So, when someone searches a keyword related to your business, voilà, there you are, right at the top!

There's plenty of platforms to choose from, each with its unique flavor. Google Ads, the granddaddy of them all, focuses on keyword targeting. On the other hand, platforms like Facebook or Instagram Ads, are more about finding that niche audience based on demographics, interests, or behaviors. The key is to know where your audience hangs out and meet them there.

Now, let's talk money. Setting a budget might seem daunting, but it's about understanding your limits and goals. Start small, experiment, learn, and then scale. And as you invest, keep a keen eye on the return on investment (ROI). It's not just about how much you spend, but how effectively you spend it. Are you getting leads? Conversions? Brand awareness? Measure, tweak, and optimize.

Star Collaborators of the Digital Age

In the shimmering realm of digital marketing, two stars have been steadily on the rise, casting their radiant glow on brands eager to shine: Influencer and Affiliate Marketing. These aren't just buzzwords; they're game-changing strategies that, when harnessed correctly, can propel your brand into the limelight.

Let's start with influencer marketing. Think of it as word-of-mouth marketing, but turbocharged. Influencers, be they celebrities, experts, or even that girl-next-door with a killer fashion sense, have a dedicated following that listens, engages, and most importantly, trusts them. This trust is gold. When an influencer raves about your product or showcases it in their daily routine, their followers take note, and voilà, your brand gets a stamp of approval.

But here's the trick: not every influencer is right for your brand. It's like matchmaking; you want someone who aligns with your brand's ethos, aesthetics, and audience. Dive deep into their content, understand their audience demographics, and gauge their engagement quality. Once you've spotted your match, it's time to woo them. Crafting influencer partnerships isn't just about sending free products and hoping for a shoutout. Design a mutually beneficial agreement, outline deliverables, set expectations, and ensure both parties are clear on the terms.

Now, let's pivot to affiliate marketing, the strategy where everyone wins. Imagine this: You partner with individuals or entities, they promote your product, and for every sale made through their unique link, they earn a commission. It's performance-based, meaning you only shell out when actual sales happen.

Setting up an affiliate program might sound daunting, but with the right tools and platforms, it's a breeze. Outline the commission structure, decide on the payout methods, and provide your affiliates with all they need, from unique tracking links to promotional materials. The beauty of affiliate marketing is its scalability. Whether you have ten or ten thousand affiliates, the model remains efficient.

But remember, while these strategies can amplify your reach and drive sales, they thrive on authenticity. Choose influencers who genuinely resonate with your brand, and foster genuine relationships with your affiliates. After all, in the world of marketing, authenticity isn't just a strategy; it's the soul that makes your brand unforgettable.

Podcasting Pioneers

From morning commutes to evening jogs, from cooking sessions to bedtime wind-downs, the melodious strains of podcasts have become a comforting background score to many lives. As a small business owner, this isn't just an interesting cultural shift; it's a golden opportunity knocking at your door.

Imagine sitting by a campfire, the flames casting a warm glow, as someone narrates an enthralling story. That's the essence of podcasts. They're intimate, personal, and forge a connection that few other mediums can claim. Now, how can your business tap into this magic?

If you've got stories to tell, insights to share, or a unique perspective that the world needs to hear, starting your own podcast might just be your calling. But here's the trick: Don't make it a blatant advertisement platform. No one wants to listen to a 30-minute sales pitch. Instead, offer value.

Find Your Unique Voice: Maybe it's interviews with industry experts, behind-the-scenes looks into your business, or discussions on topics close to your brand's heart. Find a niche that resonates with your audience.

Engage & Involve: Run contests, invite listener questions, or even have occasional guest appearances from loyal customers. Make your listeners feel like they're part of a community.

Consistency is Key: Like any content platform, regularity matters. Whether it's weekly, bi-weekly, or monthly, find a rhythm and stick to it.

If starting your own show feels daunting, fret not! Advertising on popular podcasts can be just as effective. But here's where you need to tread with finesse. Your approach shouldn't scream "advertiser"; instead, it should humbly whisper "fan."

Choose Wisely: Pick a podcast that aligns with your brand values and appeals to your target demographic. It's not just about the number of listeners but about the right listeners.

Be Genuine: When reaching out, express genuine admiration for their content. Share specific episodes or moments you loved. This sets the stage for a collaborative partnership rather than a transactional deal.

Offer Value to Listeners: Instead of a generic ad spot, can you offer special discounts to the podcast's listeners? Or perhaps sponsor a segment that aligns with your brand? Think of ways to integrate seamlessly into the show.

Leverage Host Endorsements: Podcast hosts often have a loyal following that trusts their recommendations. A personal endorsement, where the host shares their positive experience with your product or service, can be incredibly impactful.

Engage on Social Platforms: Comment on their episodes, share their content, and engage in discussions. This not only puts you on their radar but also fosters genuine relationships.

Attend Live Shows or Webinars: Many podcasters host live shows or webinars. Attend these, ask insightful questions, and network.

Collaborate on Content: Can you co-create a special episode or a series? Or maybe run a joint contest? Collaborative efforts often yield the most authentic results.

Metrics & Melodies

In marketing there's a silent observer measuring every move, every leap, every spin. This observer? Analytics. Welcome to the world of measuring marketing success, where numbers and creativity waltz in harmony.

In the world of marketing, without analytics, you're driving blind. Data-driven decisions are the compass that guide you, ensuring every marketing dollar and effort is steered in the right direction.

Now, you might wonder, "With the vast ocean of data out there, where do I even begin?" The answer: Tools for tracking marketing performance. From Google Analytics to HubSpot, these tools are like your trusty co-pilots, offering insights into website traffic, user behavior, conversion rates, and so much more. They help decode the story your numbers are telling.

We discussed Key Performance Indicators (KPIs) already earlier in the book and they also play a crucial role in evaluating the success of a marketing campaign. Think of KPIs as the pulse points of your marketing efforts. Whether it's the click-through rate of an email campaign, the conversion rate of a landing page, or the engagement on a social media post, KPIs offer a snapshot of your marketing health. But remember, while KPIs are crucial, they aren't one-size-fits-all. Tailor them to align with your business goals and objectives.

Ever heard of the butterfly effect? The idea that a tiny tweak can lead to significant results? In marketing, this magic is captured through A/B testing. By testing two versions of a campaign, be it different headlines, images, or call-to-actions, you can pinpoint what resonates best with your audience. It's like having a crystal ball, giving you a glimpse into what works and what doesn't.

Lastly, adaptability is your superpower. As you dive into data, you'll uncover insights, revelations, and sometimes, surprises. Embrace them. Refine your strategies, optimize campaigns, and always, always keep learning.

Chapter Fifteen

The Art and Science of Business Expansion

Spotting the Signs for Expansion

In the journey of nurturing a business, it often starts as a delicate seedling, needing constant care and attention. But as time rolls on, that little seedling grows, reaching new heights and spreading its branches. It's a captivating sight, watching your creation evolve and thrive. And just as a plant might outgrow its pot, hinting at the need for a new home, your burgeoning business can show signs of needing a more expansive playground.

Think of the growth trajectory of your business like that favorite shirt you've worn for years. At first, it fits just right, but over time, you start to feel it stretching at the seams, perhaps hinting that it's time for a change. Similarly, your enterprise might be giving off gentle nudges, suggesting it's ripe for the next big leap.

One of the earliest signs is the consistent buzz of activity, with demands for your product or service skyrocketing. Imagine the joy when orders flood in, products fly off the shelves, and you're swamped in the best possible way. When this pace becomes the norm, and you're perennially racing to keep up, it's nature's way of saying there's a bigger market out there, eager for what you've got.

Of course, dreams and passion are vital, but the true lifeblood of any business? Cold hard numbers. If those numbers have been painting a vibrant picture, with profits soaring and cash flow steady, it's a testament to your venture's robust health. Expansion, while thrilling, is also a gamble. But with a robust financial backbone, it's a calculated risk, one taken with the confidence that the odds are in your favor.

But what's a ship without its crew? A business, too, leans heavily on its team. If you sense an electric charge in the air every time you step into your workspace, it's more than just static. It's the pulsating energy of a team raring to go, hinting they're geared up for grander challenges. When targets aren't just met but consistently surpassed, when brainstorming sessions become whirlwinds of groundbreaking ideas, you know you've got a crew that's not just on board but eagerly manning the sails, ready to journey into deeper waters.

Navigating the Challenges of Expansion: Preparing for the Uncharted Waters

Every entrepreneur dreams of the day their business grows beyond its initial boundaries. Yet, as with every great adventure, expansion isn't just about riding the waves of success—it's also about skillfully navigating the stormy seas of challenge and uncertainty.

One of the first challenges a growing business faces is resource allocation. As demand increases, there's a temptation to throw every available resource at it. But beware! Over-expanding without a strategic plan can strain your resources thin. Expanding your team, space, or product line requires a delicate balance: ensuring you have enough to meet demand, but not so much that you're left with unsold stock or idle hands.

Then there's the challenge of maintaining your company's core values and culture. As businesses grow, they often bring in new team members, expand to new locations, or even diversify into new markets. In the midst of this whirlwind, it's easy for the original essence—the very soul of your business—to get diluted. Remember that game of 'Chinese whispers' we played as kids? The more people in the chain, the more the original message changed. In the same way, as your business family grows, ensuring everyone is aligned with your core values becomes crucial.

Increased operational demands are another aspect of the expansion maze. While yesterday's systems and processes might have been perfect for a smaller scale, today's expanded operations might outgrow them. This is the time to invest in robust systems, be it CRM tools, advanced analytics, or even automated production lines, ensuring your operations run as smoothly as a well-oiled machine.

Quality control, ahoy! When you're a small business, monitoring the quality of your products or services is like keeping an eye on a puddle. But as you grow, this puddle can become an ocean. Expansion often leads to increased production, and without stringent quality checks, this could result in compromised standards. It's essential to ramp up your quality control mechanisms, ensuring that your business reputation remains untarnished.

Lastly, while the horizon of expansion looks alluring, it's essential to remember that every new territory comes with its own set of challenges. Whether it's understanding a new market's cultural nuances, complying with regional regulations, or even grappling with different time zones—a growing business must be agile, adaptable, and ever-ready to learn.

Wrapping up, remember that expansion is more than just scaling up operations or branching out. It's an evolution, a shift in mindset. It's about recognizing opportunities, trusting the journey, and having the audacity to dream bigger. As you stand on this thrilling precipice, ready to leap into the expansive horizon, remember to trust the journey, cherish the memories, and always, always keep an eye out for the next big adventure. After all, every end is a new beginning.

Conclusion: From Dreamer to Doer

As we turn the final pages of this guide, I invite you to pause, reflect and celebrate the entrepreneurial expedition we've undertaken together. From the spark of an idea to crafting a flourishing empire, the journey of entrepreneurship is nothing short of a thrilling adventure.

We began our quest by embracing the entrepreneurial spirit, understanding the highs and lows of this rollercoaster ride. Recognizing opportunities, validating golden ideas, and choosing the right oceans for our business ventures set the stage for our voyage. But with every adventure comes its fair share of ghosts and ghouls. We tackled fears head-on, debunked myths, and built resilience, ensuring that our entrepreneurial ship is unsinkable.

The blueprint of our business kingdom required meticulous planning. With the right funding sources, a sizzling business plan, and the perfect structure, we laid the bricks for our castle. But what's a castle without its unique charm? We delved deep into the magical marketplace, crafting products and services that aren't just solutions but spells that enchant our audience.

Positioning ourselves in the vast business galaxy, we learned to shine bright, creating our unique constellation that stands out amidst a myriad of stars. And as we ventured into the marketing realm, our strategies evolved from traditional tales to digital sagas.

But a business isn't just about the past or the present; it's a time machine that needs to be future-ready. We explored the signs of expansion, ensuring that our business not only adapts to change but thrives amidst it.

Every chapter in this book is a testament to the spirit of entrepreneurship – a blend of passion, perseverance, and a pinch of magic. But remember, while this book may conclude, your business story is just beginning. With the tools, strategies, and insights you've garnered, you're not just prepared; you're unstoppable.

Entrepreneurship is not a destination; it's a journey. And with every challenge you conquer, every goal you achieve, and every milestone you celebrate, you're not just building a business; you are living and building a dream.

Here's to you, the dreamer, the doer, the entrepreneur. May your business always thrive, and may your story inspire generations to come.

Cheers to your ever-evolving business odyssey!